Words of praise for *Feel Me Brave...*

"The slow, inevitable loss of a three-year-old, doomed to die within one year, is an almost unbearable tragedy for the loved ones left behind. In *Feel Me Brave*, such a story is voiced through the prose diary of Ryland's mother, Jessica, and the poetry of his grandfather, Walter. Their pain sears its audience because it is, with obvious difficulty, reined in, controlled, releasing just enough grief to allow the readers to cry with Ryland's loved ones. As Walter writes, such an early death is 'a fatal affront to our expectations,' his verse—unsentimental, sometimes angry—is always saturated with love. Ryland's mother, Jessica, manages to convey the courage of her parents and husband and daughter, Ryland's sibling, while trying to wade through the sorrow of letting go of her child, as he finally dies in her arms."

—Laura Claridge, author of *Norman Rockwell* and *Emily Post*

"Jessica and Walter connect with the hearts and minds of everyone who must consider serious challenges in life's course, who struggle with intractable sadness and want to understand what is happening and why. Their words, both simple and elegant, wrap us into the love and mystery in day-to-day events and transcendent moments as they both seek meaning and the courage to persevere. We can all empathize deeply and learn fully from the story they have been generous enough to share."

—James R. Everett, M.D.
Medical Director, Hospice of the South Shore, Weymouth, Massachusetts

"As you begin reading *Feel Me Brave*, you just may sense something like a voice saying those mythic words, 'take off your shoes, you are on sacred ground.' It is very, very rare that words can do what this book does. Jessica and Walter offer this gift to the rest of us. It comes by some miracle of having the capacity for such profound mindfulness, and because these words are written not in hindsight, or from theory, but from deep within the experience. If you are involved in health care, or any form of ministry, psychotherapy, or if you find yourself in need of insight with regard to what the experience of losing a child entails, you will be grateful for this book. And if you, dear one, find yourself in the midst of your own experience, this book will 'hold a lamp to light your way.'"

—Reverend Daniel Jantos, North Chapel Universalist Society

"Reading this extraordinary work has impressed me that, in Walter's words, 'kindness, courage and love are all that matters' and 'that kindness is sorrow's sweet offshoot.' We are all flawed, imperfect, cracked vessels. We know it, and like Ryland, we all wonder 'Mom will I ever be able to ride my bike by myself?' What we need to hear is not 'yes', but Jess's answer, 'I don't know, but we will always be here to help you.' Thank you both for laboring on such a hard and priceless work.

I am sure it helped you heal, and I know it can help others."

— Jack van Hoff
  Section Chief of Pediatric Hematology/Oncology at Dartmouth-Hitchcock Clinic
  Lebanon, New Hampshire

"The haunting portrait of a family who suffers the unthinkable, rendered with devastating honesty and grace, *Feel Me Brave* is also a gorgeous, strangely incandescent meditation on the mysteries of faith, love, and loss, and a moving testament to the transformative power of art."

—Dawn Tripp, author of *Game of Secrets* and *Georgia: a Novel of Georgia O'Keeffe*

"'Be careful, everyone.' Uttered in a moment of worry and offered as an admonition and instruction, these are Ryland's words of wisdom that must be taken to heart on every level. In sharing his story, Jess and Walter invite readers to 'be careful' in the ways this magical little boy taught them: Be careful to love and live every day with your whole being. Be careful to see each and every day of your life (no matter its length) as full and complete. Be careful to allow both your grief and your hope in as companions. Be careful to remember the entirety of the loved one who left you too soon—not just the highest highs and the lowest lows—but the entire arc of that sacred life. And be careful to remain open to all the ways in which your beloved will ever remain with you on your journey."

—Rev. Kristine Bowen, M.Div., BCC, Staff Chaplain
  Children's Hospital at Dartmouth-Hitchcock Medical Center

Feel Me Brave

Feel Me Brave

A Chronicle of Illness, Loss, and Living Beyond

JESSICA STOUT

WALTER HORAK

DEDICATION...

For Ryland
And the many other children who,
So remarkably present and true in their too brief lives,
Remind us to be
More fully human in our own.

FOREWORD

by Ira Byock, M.D.

How brave are you? It is said that courage is not an absence of apprehension, but the reflex or resolve to do something important in spite of one's fear. Well, this book is important. Its beauty will draw you in and move you. Such is the power of authentic literature and art.

But you have to be brave to read it.

Let me ask another, related question: If forced to choose, would you rather live happily or deeply? If you answered happily, without equivocation, put down this book. It's not for you. For this is a soulful exploration of sadness. However, if you said "deeply," without equivocation, then you hold in your hands a treasure. How lucky you are to have found it.

This is a love story. Through Jessica's authentic prose voice and the lyric emotional imagery of Walter's poems, *Feel Me Brave* brings to life a little boy who lit up a family. Ryland shows us what bravery is all about. Jess and Walter show us the possibility of keeping one's heart open even while grief tears it apart.

Feel Me Brave may teach you important things about yourself; not all of which you wanted to know. Oh, I don't mean anything shameful or embarrassing; quite the contrary. It is likely to teach you about your capacity to love in the face of loss. These journal entries and poems reveal love and grief to be photo-negatives of one another. In grief we stare at the bright shadows for an image of our beloved.

More than once I thought about Alfred Lord Tennyson's poem, *In Memoriam A.H.H.* Reeling with grief over the death of a dear friend, Tennyson opined,

> 'Tis better to have loved and lost
> Than never to have loved at all.

True enough. Resoundingly true. Still the pain demands its due.

The people in his life loved Ryland so thoroughly and joyfully that his diagnosis was an emotional dagger to the familial chest. Piercing, breath-taking, when the pain subsided to an ache, it felt like welcome relief. His disease and death foretold drained his parents, sister, and grandparents. Still, Ryland was a gift in their lives.

Every life is a whole life with a beginning, middle and ending. Some are more compressed than others. Ryland lived a full life. He had joys and triumphs, and much pain, loss and sadness. He never lost his love of others, nor apparently, his pixyish humor. He died in the arms of the people who loved him into this world. Without romanticizing his absence, Ryland is indelibly written into the unfolding history of his family.

This hauntingly poetic memoir is ultimately uplifting. It answers core life questions few of us have the courage to ask: Yes! It is more important to live deeply and love completely than to avoid pain.

That brings me back to you, the one who is reading these words in contemplation of reading this book. Good for you. Know this: Empathy makes us fully human, yet it comes with a cost. Be gentle and generous with yourself while reading this book. Take your time. Allow yourself to cry. Remember to breathe and, with Jess and Walter as your guides, keep your heart open.

Allow the story to work on you. It won't make you different, just more yourself. Perhaps more confident, stronger—not in the sense of being hardened or tougher, but rather, more soulfully resilient.

So collect yourself. And when you're ready, begin.

Ira Byock, MD
Los Angeles, California
December 2014

INTRODUCTION

PARENTHOOD UNIVERSALLY ushers in surprises, discoveries, unforeseen challenges and delights. With that said, my initial experience as a parent seemed to fit within the bounds of "normal" expectations. Even with the perilous delivery of our second child, my husband and I ultimately found ourselves grateful and content with a healthy daughter, Jane, and son, Ryland, roughly two years apart as planned.

Our life course changed dramatically, however, soon after Ryland's second birthday. We observed subtle yet progressing weakness on his left side and following the advice of his pediatrician, we brought him to the hospital where an MRI revealed the cause as a Diffuse Intrinsic Pontine Glioma, a tumor in the brainstem. This was a devastating discovery, as the prognosis for DIPG is poor: Most children die within nine to twelve months and very few survive past two years. The location in the brainstem threatens vital functions and renders this tumor inoperable. Treatment choices are limited and non-curative, and the typical progression of this disease and the way it steals functioning cast a horrifying shadow over the future.

Clearly, my husband and I had had altogether different plans for our future as a family. We had moved to Vermont with the intention of creating a healthy lifestyle with strong connections to nature and the outdoors. As parents we made choices with the overarching goals of security and stability for the family. I suppose that from this place of deliberate planning came a certain assumption that life would unfold in a way that aligned, at least loosely, to our vision. This vision stretched well beyond our home. It included relationships with extended family members who were experiencing the joy of welcoming first grandchildren into the family fold. Certainly for these loved ones too, there was a powerful vision for how this chapter of life should look: joyful visits and holidays together, a steady parade of milestones to witness and celebrate, from walking to biking to reading to hitting a baseball. We also had close friendships with other young families, and in those relationships too were the shared expectations of many fun times together and the hope for lasting bonds between our children.

So this relatively small yet overwhelmingly powerful tumor struck our family at its core, with a profound and far-reaching impact outward. We were all faced with the deep despair of losing dear

Ryland—a child, a brother, a grandchild, a nephew, a friend—and had all experienced a sudden and violent assault both on our expectations and our sense of safety and justice in the world. Torn apart as we were, we nonetheless set out on a mission to care for Ryland as best we could. Medically, my husband and I elected to pursue a standard treatment course of radiation, as well as a clinical trial in Pittsburgh, which required travel from Vermont every three weeks for vaccine injections. Our goal was to try to extend life without unduly compromising its quality, and truth be told, I was holding out hope for a miracle all along the way.

Packing for one of the many trips to Pittsburgh, I asked Ryland if he wanted to bring a special doll that had been given to him by a fellow mom in my community (just one of countless acts of kindness that helped fuel our spirits). Though he had sophisticated language for his age, Ryland responded with one of those wonderful grammatical creations that only toddlers can come up with: "Yes, feel me brave," he said. Anticipating the challenges of this trip (namely, the painful shots that he endured), little Ryland was proposing that this doll would provide comfort and courage, would help him feel brave.

Throughout this journey with a fatal illness, we would all need to feel our way to bravery. We would all need to face and endure experiences and emotions that brought us to the most dark and painful depths I have known. There was no medical solution to be found, no rational explanation to hold on to. Rather, we would need to follow our little boy's lead into the dark and aspire to his example of courage.

What follows is a pair of parallel writings that chronicles this journey. My writings, as mother, are in narrative form. In the first part, they come from a blog I maintained to communicate with concerned family and friends. In the second, the writings transition from the blog to private journaling I did after Ryland's death. The third and final part is a shorter collection of writings that reflect on how one might continue to live fully in the aftermath of profound grief.

Side by side with my pieces are the works of poetry by my father who, like myself, felt compelled to witness and give testimony to what was, and what remains, the most painful experience of our lives. Neither of us is a writer by trade, but throughout this experience we both found the written word profoundly cathartic. Neither of us set out to make a book, but in the end this father and daughter accounting cohered in a way that felt a bit like a destined love story about a boy who will always inspire.

Ours is not the first story of loss and grief, but we do hope to offer something valuable in these open-hearted words about suffering, love, and the possibility of healing from unimaginable anguish. We hope that the "real time" nature of this writing captures aspects of human emotional experience that time or recollection might miss. We hope that this testimony might in some way help others in similar straits, might inform and give insight to those in medical or care-taking positions, and might resonate with any fellow human beings who may want to meditate a bit on heartbreak (which after all is universal to our species) and in so doing feel their own way to bravery.

Jessica Stout

Illness

Journey

A young boy can walk up only a little hill
Before having to turn
And walk back down.
Along the way he sings a song
More deep and pure
Than the songs of men
Who climb mountains.

November 1...

THIS FIRST JOURNAL ENTRY needs to do a bit of catch-up, as we have all been through a lot before getting this blog up and running. And I feel like I cannot possibly capture everything. There was of course the hospital admission chapter: Post diagnosis, Ryland endured constant monitoring and assessments, and also had a port put in his chest. We somehow endured, if you can call it that, the most painful news a parent can receive: that your child has an illness with no cure. It is a grief too big to contain really, as the tears flow continuously. And there are no real answers to the "why" questions. This is a cancer with apparently no genetic or environmental cause—a random act of violence that has rendered our old life unrecognizable.

Then there was the transition home, to a new reality. The side effects of the steroids ramped up, and Ryland became more irritable and prone to meltdowns, manically hungry, and pretty much sleepless at night. He was inactive, wanting mostly to lie down on his parents. Throughout all this he also showed much affection and love, and somehow retained just enough of his amazing humor to keep us all going. We understood that the steroids were keeping him stable (i.e. the difficulty swallowing he showed at the hospital improved fairly quickly).

Ryland began radiation treatment at Dartmouth-Hitchcock Medical Center in Lebanon, New Hampshire on September 27. The beginning was very difficult. He has to be put under every time (five days a week) and cannot eat or drink in the morning hours beforehand. Not an easy task for a two-year old who was hardly sleeping at night and constantly hungry. But all in all he has rallied like a major champ. They are able to put him under in the waiting area in his daddy's arms (after checking out the fish and the motorcycle magazine). Initially, he had a brutal time coming out of anesthesia, probably related to the fact that he could not effectively sleep it off due to the steroids. This has improved greatly with steroid reduction.

Every two weeks we stay on to do an infusion of Avastin and meet at length with the oncologist. Ryland has been amazing with that, snuggling with mommy in a big chair. Overall, we have seen remarkable improvement: his gait is looking more normal, he has much better function in the left arm and hand, and he has gone from slurred/ limited speech to being very chatty and clear with his language. He is up on his feet now and playful, and seems to relish in his mobility. Today he was taken off steroids altogether (perhaps he will start the day a little past 4 a.m.?)

Sister Jane, age four, has been incredible. Of course I ache for her that she must go through this, but she has shown great strength and patience, and her honest questions and beautiful thoughts and images she shares suggest that she may be a guiding light for the grownups in some ways. We all, of course, are buoyed up by the tremendous love from family and friends (even strangers).

Leader

Keeping loved ones from harm:
A father's most daunting task.
No more so than when a daughter,
Herself a mother of a stricken child,
Asks, "Daddy, how do I bear the unbearable?"
And he has no reply.
So now with her unbearable burden,
She must answer her own question
And in so doing,
Show her father the way.

November 5...

BIG DAY FOR RYLAND, as we did lunch in Hanover and attended the Dartmouth football game with pals. He seems to share his dad's affection for the game. Not so long ago, we could not have imagined a day like this for him and the family, so quite the breakthrough. Such a beautiful fall day too. There may have even been a few purely happy moments for the parents also—though much of the time happiness or progress is weighted down by the foreboding of a grim prognosis, by how impermanent and fleeting these good times may be. I don't know whether it's a psychic tug-of-war or a balancing act between facing the reality of what medical statistics say and the hope for something miraculous for Ryland.

This tumor is very rare, though there are other brave children fighting this fight. This experience has certainly opened our eyes to a world of struggle and suffering. The injustice of it quickly gets under your skin, to learn of these young innocent souls up against something so cruel. And as you learn the stories, you hear the themes about these kids—about their kindness and bravery, selflessness and love. All the things the world needs more of.

Ryland is no exception. He has had the qualities of an old soul from the start. I remember him smiling responsively at a very young age, and generally being very connected emotionally. He has always been very affectionate and loving. When he was a little over one year old, he was the boy in music class looking out for the younger kids, making sure they had an instrument to play. Oftentimes when he receives something yummy to eat, he looks to share it with someone. He also has long had a sense of humor way beyond his years.

And of course his is a story of triumph and survival, after the birth experience. After being stuck in the birth canal for seven minutes, he was born without a heartbeat, no breathing. After two minutes he was brought back, though we were told he would have profound impairments. As the hours in the intensive care nursery went by, he made these incredible strides, which ultimately earned him the name "miracle baby" amongst the staff. In the end, he only sustained nerve strain in the right arm, for which we have done physical therapy ever since. That arm is doing fabulously (and ironically, had to become the dominant functioning side when the left started to go).

There has not been one day since his birth that I haven't thought about it and felt a deep rush of gratitude that he lived and thrived. I remember joking with him as a newborn that he cashed in all his worry chips up front, that he owed his parents some long smooth sailing. Little did I know.

After he fought so hard to be here, I see no place for a terminal disease. So I say, let the miracle baby do it again.

Son-in-law

My son-in-law is a big man,
A strong man,
A man of accomplishments so remarkable,
That some no doubt believe
He can leap tall buildings in a single bound.
Yet the crucible of grief and pain
Where he currently resides
Is the thing that will define him forevermore.
I watch
As he hands his limp, sleeping son to the doctors
And see the mix
Of strength and despair in his eyes.
I watch again
As his son revives in an angry temper
And marvel
At his patient ministrations.
For all his prior good deeds,
I am now witness to
A new aspect of him:
A reservoir within
From which daily mercies and kindnesses
Flow gently to a suffering family,
And in that I see
The full measure of the man.

November 8...

THIS WAS RYLAND'S FINAL DAY OF RADIATION. In some ways it's hard to believe we're here already, thinking back to how daunting the six weeks felt going into it. How would we deprive him of food and water every morning of the week? How could we put him under each time? How would we deny him and his sister bath time together (a favorite activity) because he has a tube dangling from his chest that can't get wet? Somehow all those things were surmounted. Matt deserves enormous credit for bringing Ryland each time, sometimes with me or another family member, but other times on his own. It is a wrenching thing to watch your son go to sleep in your arms and then surrender him, limp and vulnerable, to the team. It is an emotional and tearful walk out of that room. But Matt handled that with a stunning combination of tenderness and strength that I know gave great comfort to Ryland, not to mention me.

The team too quickly earned our trust and confidence with a combination of professionalism and personal, human care that seems to be a consistent strength of the Dartmouth approach to medicine. They had goodbye presents for Ryland today, for goodness sake. I did get the sense that this was deeply moving for them, to be treating a small child in his zip-up pajamas who appeared to be a good seventy years younger than the average person in the waiting room.

Finally, Ryland of course was a champion in his willingness to do what needed to be done. There was perhaps the advantage too of the toddler mind: being in the moment, being able to move on from the tough moments to something better, finding comfort in routine. Honestly, he will probably miss that early morning drive in some ways, checking to see what diggers are at work (and we have a lot of those after Hurricane Irene), checking to see what balloons are up at the car dealerships.

As a parent, I guess what I will "miss" is the feeling of having a plan, the feeling of being proactive, and the semblance of control. After this standard recommended treatment, there is no real common path for families to travel—it becomes much more of an individual journey based on the child and on the parents' judgment of what seems "right." I know for us we want to prioritize his quality of life, and at the same time consider whatever is out there to extend life expectancy with a minimum of compromise. We are considering a clinical trial in Pittsburgh involving a vaccine/immunotherapy approach.

We wouldn't have to move there, but it does involve frequent travel. From what we can tell, the risks in terms of side effects seem quite minimal compared to other chemo approaches, though he would need regular injections and MRIs. A big decision. When I think of Pittsburgh I think of the one time I went there to look at Carnegie Mellon with my dad when I was trying to figure out where to go to college (remember that trip, Dad?). To think of what a big decision that felt like at the time! It makes my own life feel pretty long, to be looking at Pittsburgh again under these very different circumstances, with the stakes infinitely higher. Tomorrow night we talk to the lead doctor out there, and hopefully that will provide more clarity about where to go from here.

Morning/Mourning

Each dark morning my grandson's anguished cry
Is now sweet to the ear,
A reassuring sign of a beat in the heart
And also a reminder
Of the boy's perilous beginning,
Born with neither pulse nor breath.
He was a miracle then
And so each morning
He will continue to be,
Even as he struggles with his infirmities
And each new day alternately plods and races.
He turns to me now
And I consider the life and love in his eyes.
I return his look
With my own boundless affection,
Hoping that my despair does not give me away.

November 13...

IT'S LOOKING LIKE we're going to pursue the clinical trial in Pittsburgh. We had an informative conversation with the doctor the other night, and felt that the treatment approach is quite compelling. As opposed to traditional chemo drugs, which have not shown significant effectiveness and which tend to impose side effects and risks, this is a vaccine aimed at training the body to fight the tumor. It involves two injections each time we go, (every three weeks for six months, then every six weeks until progression of tumor or up to two years). They will also do regular MRIs in Pittsburgh to monitor the tumor.

The drawbacks are: pain from the injections (this will not be pleasant for a two-year old), flu-like symptoms for a day or so, and then the potential for swelling, which is perhaps the most concerning as we could see some deterioration in functioning and may need to resume steroids to some extent. It seems like kids vary a bit in how they respond, so we won't know until we try (and can of course stop at any time if it doesn't seem worth it). No one is saying the word cure here, and this is quite a novel approach with this diagnosis. But it does allow for some hope for at least an extension of life, which may open other doors down the road. Ryland will be the youngest child in the trial by a couple years.

Ryland continues to have happy days right now. He is savoring life and seems to be developing at a high speed lately. Soon after discharge from the hospital, he insisted on sleeping in the twin bed in his room—no more crib, skipped the toddler bed altogether. Once he got his speech back, his language has been on fire...more sophisticated words and sentences, asking what words mean, always deciphering and trying to understand. And he talks about being a big boy a lot. He recently insisted he was in high school. Watching the high school football team practice the other day, he begged to join in, with complete confidence that he would hold his own. He also seems to be one-upping his sister these days with the teasing skills——his slick humor tends to put me in stitches before I get it together to be a semi-decent arbiter with the siblings.

We hope that his life will continue to have this happy and exciting flavor for some time, even if we do gear up for the travel and interventions involved with the trial. A few weeks ago I would have guessed we wouldn't do the trial, as we so want him to have a good, normal-ish life while he is doing better. I am hoping we can still give him that to a large extent, and that he will respond well to the treatment.

One last thing and that is to thank everyone out there who has been so supportive in various ways—for your messages and cards, your thoughts and prayers. I wish I could thank you all personally and I probably never will get around to writing notes (which I typically enjoy doing). Just know that we are so grateful for the family and friends we have and for all the love that has been pouring in.

Dinner Out

The child's angry outbursts
Drew reproachful looks
From the other diners,
An understandable reaction
If it were a matter
Of simple bad behavior
And not the outward manifestation
Of a fiendish malignancy in the boy's brain.
As we fled the restaurant, his grandmother for the record
Set them straight,
And, if there's a god of gastronomy,
Induced with her words
A bout of poor digestion
From their gourmet meals.

November 16...

THE TRIAL WILL START IN MID-DECEMBER. So these next few weeks we plan to savor some quiet days at home and also take a trip out to Park City to see Matt's family. This will be Ryland's first time out there, and he is excited, asking daily now if it's time to get on the airplane.

I am hoping the trip will provide some escapism for all of us—maybe denial will have a chance to work better in new surroundings. Because otherwise, life is pretty heavy. The Pittsburgh doctor described his tumor as the "worst of the worst" of pediatric cancers. We've been hearing dire things all along, but you do start to hope someone can put a slightly different spin on it. With these words rattling around in my head, I thought I would exorcise a few more thoughts here (reader beware, I guess).

It all begs the question—how did we get here? Three months ago, a broken leg would have seemed pretty horrible. And I think back to the super healthy pregnancies, the natural childbirths, nursing Ryland until he was two, the organic food, the BPA-free plastics, etc., etc.—all those things you do out of a drive to protect and yet still—the worst of the worst happens. I suppose there has been plenty of evidence in my life, his birth in particular, that demonstrate the limits of one's control and best laid plans. (Hey universe—I get it! or at least leave my kid out of this.) Still, I assumed that I would have kids and watch them grow, and pass away before them according to a natural order of things. Perhaps that was not my assumption to make, that in fact when you bring forth a love of this magnitude, you create vulnerability and the potential for pain in the same measure.

And it is beyond measure. The grief is in every cell of our bodies. We feel ancient and hurt and ache in ways we don't recognize. I like to fantasize that in fact, my body feels this way because my visualizations of inhaling the tumor out of Ryland to do battle with it myself are working.

We will never know "why" and can only figure out how to respond, which I know is a long, shifting process. Going with the current seems to be the only way, and so far this seems to mean getting slammed against various rocks most of the time but also some moments of calm too. The happy times with Ryland possess an acute sense of pain about losing him, his cute little face and voice and way about him. You try to live in the moment, which parenthood helps to teach, but you soon realize how much projecting you actually do. You watch your son swing a bat and think about Little League with him (and now, the possibility of not having that). And the holidays of course now have that weight of, "Is this the last…?"

In all of this there are these rare and fleeting, yet real moments of peace and focus. I don't know how or why they come—not much rhyme or reason—but they are like taking a breath before going back down under water. I am hoping for more of those with time.

December 5...

WE ARE BACK FROM A GREAT TRIP to Grandma's house in Park City. Ryland proved to be an excellent traveler. He saw big mountains and lots of family on Daddy's side, including his three great-grandparents. It was wonderful to connect with everyone out there and in many cases introduce Ryland for the first time.

Since returning home, Ryland has done a couple mornings at his old school. A month ago, this would have seemed like a major stretch, so it is exciting. Of course, it is hard for the mind not to travel farther back to when he started this school in June: He was active and vibrant and content with a quick kiss goodbye before he confidently set forth into the school scene. He is now a bit timid, a bit anxious for Mom to stick around, and his physical weaknesses stand out more when amongst his peers. So that contrast can feel like a real stab to the heart—seeing what has been taken from him, and no longer feeling "normal." But you redefine success, and while he may struggle more with things, you know that his soul still shines.

In the same way that the tumor is "diffuse" and "intrinsic" amongst healthy cells, so too is it in our daily life and activities—always there, always intensifying everything or adding perspective or adding a weight of sadness that can feel crushing. I'm not sure if I'll have one pure emotional state again. Everything is so mixed up: joy with sadness, hope with fear. You can have a moment of peace or optimism, but the rug gets pulled again and again, and the plunge into the darkness is a long one. These are tremendous depths. I look at Ryland and I still see my perfect baby. I am still overwhelmed by his beauty. And as Matt said last night, he only seems to be getting cuter and more endearing as he grows up and becomes himself. In all this beauty and promise, it is still just unthinkable that there could be something so wrong at work. It's like someone violently threw back the curtain, and we are no longer on the stage of life but wandering around back stage, bumping around in the dark, no familiar props or anticipated storyline.

Well, our new story will soon include the city of Pittsburgh, a fittingly gritty spot where we have placed all our hopes! I am feeling really good about pursuing the trial and fortunate that Ryland qualifies. He will have his first post-radiation MRI out there on December 15, followed by the first administration of the vaccine. Certainly a new spin on the holiday season! Matt and I might be spiking our 'nog' a little more this year.

Keep all that great energy coming Ryland's way. We remain so appreciative of all the support.

Plea

My grandson's warm round body
Pressed face down on mine
Is surely the closest
To a heaven I'll ever get.
Like some kind of latter day cherub
Descended from a chapel ceiling,
This morning he chose me
As an earthly slumber spot.
There the quiet sounds of our bodies merged,
Breaths, heartbeats, and gurgling bellies.
In the wake of a fleeting contentment
I make my plea:
Would that by some further, miraculous osmosis
He could pass his affliction on to me
And thereby right the outrageous wrong
Of his early death
Likely preceding mine.

December 19...

WELL, WE HAVE DONE PITTSBURGH TRIP #1. Waiting at the airport, I flipped open my recent *Newsweek* (the one with Newt Gingrich all over the cover) and thought it auspicious to find the science article on cancer vaccines being a very promising trend in treatment, with the beloved word "cure" thrown in for good measure (or maybe just to sell magazines, as I don't know how close we are to that).

I suppose the high from that article, and the rescue fantasies about this trial in general, had to be tempered eventually. We were soon up against the realities of being one of the masses in a big city hospital (we are spoiled by the square footage per patient and relative calm of Dartmouth). We had transfer of care things to iron out. And most of all, Ryland had a full day of medical challenges and a good deal of waiting. With congestion and an ear infection (uncle!), he had to be put under deeper for the MRI, which just made recovery a lot longer and tougher. He wasn't too keen on having anyone do anything to him. He persevered through the two shots (one is pretty deep), but they left him really sore and refusing to walk for a solid day. (We joke that phase two of this trial will probably administer the vaccine through chocolate cake.)

Some good news: The doctor was impressed by the effects of the radiation on the tumor. She couldn't really quantify the shrinkage, as that is apparently tricky to do, but she described good evidence of death of tumor cells. Of course, we would have loved to see it all gone, and it was hard to look at it again: his cute little profile and perfect little head and brain, except for this area that went awry for unknown reasons. It is truly unbelievable what the impact of tiny cells can be on a body, a life, a family.

And it was more than sobering to hear that the doctor did not think it was possible for the vaccine to knock out this tumor, due to the complexity and resilience of tumor cells. I guess this was not new information. And I appreciate her "realist" approach (I think). But all that effort coupled with the sense of doom coming from key places leaves you a bit beaten down.

So, in some ways we are back to where we started: still gunning for that miracle, still trying to nurture some hope to get us through our days. And that's where everyone's continued thoughts and prayers and tonglen and chants and energy and seriously, whatever suits you, factor in so strongly for me. I am so humbled by the mysteries of this universe and at the same time so very open to whatever can impart healing on my sweet boy.

Daughter

Early on in the journey
I remember observing
My daughter's son asleep in his hospital bed
And questioning in disbelief
How anyone so beautiful
Could be related to me,
An honest comment
But tinged with enough humor
To make his mother laugh,
Amid tears of grief and fear.
Months later, a disease progresses,
The child's tribulations grow daunting,
And strains on the family overwhelm.
Our world so turned upside down,
I now observe the mother,
With all her patience and courage and love,
And think what a blessing
That she is my daughter.

December 31...

It's New Year's Eve. I am very content to be at home in front of the fire with the promise of being in bed before midnight. (I guess that could describe most years lately, but this is a particularly sober night.) I am quite ready to let 2011 go, though 2012 presents so much uncertainty. Statistics and most doctors say I will lose my child this year; my will and my heart say—not without a fight. I'm not even sure what that fight really looks like. I certainly don't want it to look like desperate attempts to extend his life at the expense of his well-being. Recently this fight has felt more spiritual to me, with questions about life and death and the power of love. I have always been more of a seeker than a knower, not religiously affiliated though not agnostic. I have tended to be comfortable with the questions and the learning process, though I wonder if this experience will change any of that. I don't know. My mind just tends to be spinning at all times (which actually can make you miss Dick Clark a little bit).

Christmas was wonderful. We had a house full of family, and Ryland has been doing well. He has some lingering, mild weakness, and it is hard not to over-analyze every little bend of the finger, and eyelid droop, and catch in his step. But when I step back and look at the big picture, he is physically in pretty good shape. Emotionally, he is a bit more clingy with Mom, a little wakeful at night, moody at times. But who can blame him. It's also tricky to differentiate what is two year-old stuff and what is a result of everything he's been through. Mostly, he is still a dear, funny, twinkly little boy.

I learned of several losses of children this past month within the DIPG community, so my heart was heavy for them this Christmas, and I was very aware of how fortunate we were to have Ryland with us and doing so well. It was very difficult to hear that the child who had shown the best response on the Pittsburgh trial (in terms of longevity) passed away on Christmas day. We are so sad for her family, and we also feel plunged back into this place of doubt about what the right course is for Ryland. We meet with our hometown doctors this week to discuss his last MRI, as well as our treatment concerns.

Interesting things have happened amidst the chaos. I went to the bank the other day to sign a couple things. The woman who had been helping us before was out, so another lady stepped in. Fairly quickly, this mundane transaction with a stranger turned into an hour long, emotional conversation—

when she was six, she lost her two-year old sister to a brain stem tumor. Heavy as that sounds, our talk was ultimately very comforting, with a strong meant-to-be feeling. I also very randomly ran into my midwife today on a shopping excursion to buy Jane ballet shoes. I have been thinking about her so much, wanting her to know about Ryland but unsure how and when to tell her (I knew she was due to have a baby around the time of Ryland's diagnosis). But there she was, and it was another emotional and very meaningful exchange.

I guess these are the moments that help instill a little more trust in the universe. Here's to more of that for the New Year.

Stream

My grandson and I are sharing the couch again,
He a sleeping blanket pressed against my chest,
And at this moment
We are the center of a small universe.
Certainly the countless threads of communication
From people offering thoughts and prayers and positive energy
Suggest something of cosmic significance,
Out in faraway spaces an awakening of hearts
Radiating light back from all directions
Towards our center.

The concern is gratifying, even uplifting to a point
Where I can hope some good may come of it,
 Some extension of his life.
Yet I consider the notion of the perfect moment
Here and now, as it is,
He terminally ill and me the despairing grandpa.

Could there be something of the divine here?
Something transcendent?
Is it possible that there is a far deeper, ancient stream of energy
Also engaging us,
Flowing back and forth in time and space?
And might this stream be coursing
With the spirits of ancestors and contemporaries and descendants alike,
A current wherein all of humankind
Are dissolved and bound together?

I think I can be comforted by this idea, however inchoate,
That my grandson and I are now swimming together,
Even for just a few moments,
Immersed in infinite waters.

January 1...

I KNOW I JUST WROTE so I'll keep this brief. I went on my usual walk in the woods with my dog today (nature continues to be a reliable source of sanity and comfort for me). I went in the morning which is not typical, but I think I liked the "seize the day, seize the year" kind of feeling it gave. It was strangely warm for a January morning in Vermont; there was a spring-like feeling in the air. There has been a ton of logging up in the woods, so there was this combination of beauty and destruction all around. I arrived at the lookout spot, and for the first time of all the times I have gone there, there was a very thick bank of fog. Usually you look down the hill to the road and out to the river and the mountains beyond. Today I could just see down the hill a little ways, with two barren but beautiful trees in the center and two smaller ones off to the side. Behind that was all fog, except for way up high I could see the undulating ridge line peeking through, with the appearance of a calligrapher's brushstroke up in the sky. My first reaction was that this was the perfect "view" to start the coming year, which was essentially no view, no clarity, no firm grasp on how things will unfold. The next feeling was more surprising, as I felt a strange peace staring into this void, which started to feel less like a wall and more like a soothing force of life and motion. And there were the four trees standing out and rooted strongly, and above them, the hint of something beyond.

Gift

He wraps his son in a deep embrace
More reminiscent of a she-bear
Than the male counterpart.
Drawing him into his chest, he lowers his face
To make contact with the top of the little boy's head
And inhales deeply, eyes closed.
He revels in the scalp's aroma,
The bodily essence of his son,
A moment to make last,
Just the two alone in the world.
It occurs to me that the father may be attempting something further,
And though I can't bring myself to say it aloud,
I imagine he might be trying to aspirate the offending bit of biology
From the boy's brain,
Trying to do at least symbolically
What medicine has yet been unable to do,
Rid us of the affliction that torments us so.
The boy has been a gift from the beginning
And as his life now hangs in the balance,
I know that this gesture, this hug,
This attempt to heal,
Is the father's gift in return.

January 11...

We are back from Pittsburgh trip #2. No MRI this time, just the exam and injections, which still took up a better part of a day. Ryland struggled more with the shots this time, probably because he knew what was coming. He has also been very sore again—he had the shots on Monday afternoon, and was just starting to really walk again this evening.

I wish we didn't feel so conflicted still about the trial. It can feel like a lot to put him through without a promise of significant benefit, based on the results of the trial thus far. We worry about the potential for inflammation and the possibility of doing harm with the vaccine itself. No one can make any real solid predictions about anything, so a sense of clarity can be very elusive despite all our information gathering. Obviously, this can be pretty torturous as parents. Every fiber of your being is geared towards protecting and nurturing your child; now with a child who is considered terminally ill, we are re-channeling those impulses into trying to make the best decisions for him along the course of this disease. We are learning that this is truly a day-to-day process as we gather every bit of new information, watch how he is doing, and tune into our instincts the best we can.

Despite the hassle of travel, and our ambivalence about going to Pittsburgh in general, I experienced one of those unexpected moments of peace while there. I think this time it had something to do with being together with Matt and Ryland in a totally random place. We were taking a walk Sunday afternoon (the day before our appointments) around the hospital neighborhood. There were not that many thriving businesses or places to go, but we did find a little bookstore and went in to warm up and have a look. It was cute, with an anarchist bent, edgy-folky music playing softly. The three of us sat down on the small couch with some used books, Ryland sandwiched between us very calm and content. And there we were for a long while passing around a collection of Rumi, a Herman Melville biography, and a copy of *Everybody Poops*. All I could think of in that moment was: "This is perfect." Life feels so painful so much of the time that those fleeting moments are quite sublime.

While we love being home, I think it helped to be away, in that random place, where our connections to each other take on a kind of boundless and timeless quality. Home can be more complicated: You have the comforts, but you also have the reminders of all that you have work towards and all that you expected life to be. The hardest part is watching the sibling relationship evolve and deepen, knowing that it may be short-lived and that Jane may lose her little brother, who has become her friend and playmate. Matt and I will be finishing dinner, listening to the two of them giggle and play upstairs, and just weep into our plates. This is the psychological challenge of this stage. He is doing well and we are largely going through the motions of a "normal life" with the knowledge that he can be taken from us any time. They call the post-radiation phase, when there is a return of functioning, the "honeymoon phase." Well, we must have married a real monster if this is a honeymoon (annulment!)

One more story. We were down in Rhode Island before Pittsburgh to drop Jane off with her grandparents and spend a little time. We had beautiful, warm weather for January so I took a jog to the beach. Half way there I encountered a running race coming the opposite direction, so I moved on to the grass and kept going. There were a few friendly "wrong ways!" called out, which of course made me think instantly about my life's course, in more of a humorous way than a heavy way really. It is true, though, with illness like this—the feeling like you are going, if not in reverse, then way off course from the pack. But you must keep going in the direction that your "run" is taking you. At least for me, on that run, the destination was the beach, which could not have looked more glorious, and I was meeting up with my family. That too was sublime, perfect, with the feeling of something eternal.

Trickster

There was life before and there will be life after Ryland
But at this moment in time
His presence is so keenly felt
That giving him up looms an incomprehensible task,
Like putting the genie back in the bottle,
The cat back in the bag.
Barely with us it seems, he's made
A hopelessly big and splendid love
That is uncontainable,
That fills enormous spaces…
An exemplary trick for such a small fellow.
It occurs to me
That he's been a trickster all along,
Making treasured things up out of thin air,
Bringing down the house with a sideways glance,
Dancing a naked ballet like some latter day Pan.
He dissolves my crusty outlook with a wave of his hand,
My enchantment boundless.
No wonder I now crumble at the possibility of his loss.
How do I survive the end of the show?
Curtain closes, he vanishes,
I'll be lost without him.
Thereafter the only hope is for his traces
To pierce through my grief and deprivation:
A sweet vapor flooding this corner of the world
And a fluorescence curling cleverly
In the dark halls of my heart.

February 5...

WE HAD PITTSBURGH TRIP #3 LAST WEEK, a two-day affair this time with an MRI on Wednesday and exam/ blood draws/ injections on Thursday. The main update is that on the scan there is a new spot of color within the tumor. The doctor thinks it is most likely "leaky blood vessels" resulting from radiation, which would not be a cause for alarm. The spot seems to correspond with the most malignant part of the tumor. The other possibilities are swelling from the vaccine or tumor activity itself, which we do not want of course (she thinks this is quite unlikely). While I am feeling fairly confident that this is not an ominous change, it does give us a taste of the lack of certainty with these scans, in terms of determining exactly what color or enhancement means. Medical technology can certainly be amazing and awe-inspiring at times, though there are frustrating limits too.

Ryland continues to torture us with his cuteness and charm. Lately he enjoys performing "naked ballet," which combines his zest for nudity and his hilarious interpretations of his sister's more formal style. He also went skiing last weekend, which entails his tall daddy hunched way over to hold him up while going "really fast," as Ryland prefers. As with most activities these days, Daddy was smiling through his tears.

It struck me the other day that the average survival time with this tumor is nine months after diagnosis, the same length of a pregnancy. You are given nine months to prepare for a life, and nine months to prepare for a death. Other parallels? The nausea, the knowledge that you and your life will never be the same, and I guess the stretch marks for the latter just happen somewhere deep down in the human psyche as you try to grasp the unimaginable, and bear the unbearable.

While waiting for Ryland's MRI to finish, I opened a book that Dad had given me, one I had stopped reading after Ryland's diagnosis. Despite my fuzzy memory of what I had read, I elected to pick up where I left off, and had one of those spontaneous, meant-to-be moments as I read the content of that particular chapter. There was first of all a random historical reference to Pittsburgh of all places. But beyond that, the author, Rebecca Solnit, delves into the themes of being lost and of dramatic change in human life ("the transitions whereby you cease to be who you were"). I cannot say I have ever been a huge lover of change, but I am now deeply aware of its inevitability. And in my clearer moments, I know that the only way to survive is to surrender to change and somehow go with it. My most painful moments happen when I want to cling to the narrative that I thought was my life, Ryland's life. He has always been the survivor who fought to be here, and we have cherished his strength, smarts, beauty...and all the promise of a good life. I have frankly been in awe that he came from me...I have not been prouder of anything more than my kids. Reminds me of when my dad was watching him sleep in his hospital bed back in September and wondering aloud how someone so beautiful could be related to him.

So we put all our emotional eggs, and then some, in his basket. A vulnerable place, but the only place a parent can be. I will leave my eggs there but must somehow evolve in ways to deal with this most unexpected, agonizing turn of events. Anther quote from Solnit's book: "The process of change consists mostly of decay and then of this crisis when emergence from what came before must be total and abrupt." This is in reference to a butterfly's life cycle, but could easily describe how things feel for me: the disintegration, the loss of an old form, the need to proceed as something different. Not feeling too much like a butterfly, more like some moth of the night missing a few parts. But I guess like the moth, I must gravitate to the light, to hope, to trust in something bigger and better than fear.

Fear

I fear for my daughter's sweet family,
For the toll of all the past and present suffering.
There is an unfathomable loss that's likely to come,
And the marking of time between now and then
Seems so cruel and unusual
That I fear, above all,
How our grief will compound.

A terminal disease may very well present the gift of time,
When sufferer and caregiver can share the burden of pain and knowing,
Acknowledge the inevitable together,
And, if necessary, make amends and take stock.

But with our young boy,
There can be very little stock taking,
The arc of his life so short that we scramble
To grasp a meaningful dimension,
Barely able to imagine what might have been.
We anticipate his death as he cannot
And this seems only to amplify our pain,

That and the peculiar injustice
Of a grim fate visited on an innocent.
The inevitability that we all must share his fate
Is as yet no comfort,
And each day rends the heart: to witness
The family pursue treatment and care
That they know is likely to be futile.

It is the noblest of sacrifice,
A struggle of heroic scope,
But there's no telling how it will ravage our spirit.
Torture behind us, torture ahead,
I fear for my daughter's sweet family,
I fear for my aching loved ones,
And, after all, I fear for me.

February 27...

CAN'T QUITE CATCH MY BREATH THIS MONTH—thank goodness for the leap year, I'll have an extra day to orient myself toward March and the change of season it promises (though spring comes a little later here in Vermont). We did our "Make a Wish" trip this month, going with the well-worn Disney path. The foundation really is incredible in its dedication to children and its generosity. We stayed at GIVE KIDS THE WORLD, a resort that caters to kids with life-threatening illness. (There is some nearby land for sale, and I am thinking of developing a sister resort called GIVE THE PARENTS A DRINK. Investors welcome.) Anyway, it really was a perfect atmosphere for our kiddos... fun activities and amenities, but with a mellow, low-tech feel that proved to be a great escape from the actual theme parks, which are officially nuts. (We did have some fun for sure, but definitely more stimulation than necessary for the kids' age group.) We connected with a couple of families, but interestingly, the general tendency was to just be with your family on vacation as much as possible, without too much chatter about why we were all there. It makes for kind of a surreal pool scene—palm trees and sun, mostly happy faces, but an awareness that everyone is up against something very difficult in real life. While there was some heaviness to that, there was also something honest in the air about human suffering and mortality. Kind of an interesting juxtaposition to the plastered smiles and piped in music and "happily ever after" stuff at Disney, which didn't sit so well with me, but I'm a lost cause.

I was perhaps most moved by the story of the resort's founder, Henri Landwirth, who came to the States as a young man after being at Auschwitz as a child, where he witnessed the murder of both his parents. Somehow, he was able to work through his rage and evolve into this passionate, generous leader with a deep concern and love for children. Right now, most days, I feel like I cannot get out from under my own profound sadness, but it is definitely inspiring to think of some potential for good after horror and heartbreak.

We had another Pittsburgh trip right on the heels of Florida, which proved to be a bit much for all. It is good to now be home with some structure. Ryland is still doing well physically. He is up a lot at night, I think with some fears and nightmares sometimes. So, days don't really "end" and sleep is feeling like an unrequited love for me....but I am so grateful that he is functioning as well as he is. My fears for the future do creep in so relentlessly though, I sometimes feel like I am losing the "mind game." But you do keep moving, and I thank everyone for the fuel I find in your wise, compassionate messages.

Touch

The other night it fell to me
To put my grandson to bed,
A daunting task considering
His piled up resentment for the recent needle pokes
And the enervating effects of travel.

Pained and exasperated, he's become understandably dependent
On the comforts of his mother,
But alone with me this night he was unexpectedly quiet, calm,
And apparently trusting that I might get the pre-sleep ritual right.

For whatever reason he eschewed the books
And the usual night-time ministrations
And guided me to his dresser
And a bottle of water with a Spanish label,
Water that I remembered had been blessed by a healer in a faraway land
And brought to us by a generous friend.

Holding the boy in my arms, I followed his wordless direction:
I pour the water in a small cup, he dips his finger,
And touches first his forehead
And then the nape of his neck,
Locations that I realize form a nexus spanning the malignancy in between.
At my request he includes me in his communion,
Touching my head the same way.

The ritual is brief, seconds only, but I shudder to my soul
And wonder how we've arrived at such a dire place
Where a little boy performs his own life-saving ceremony.

Tucked in bed, he allows me to go,
And as I drift away down the hall
I find myself hoping beyond all measure
That there's something to this,
This touch of divine water.

March 27...

ANOTHER PITTSBURGH TRIP HAS COME AND GONE—they seem to come around so quickly now. The last couple of times we have elected to give Ryland a short-acting sedative for the administration of the injections. This takes the edge off his resistance and overall angst a bit and apparently acts to block his memory of it, which is probably a good thing. His physical recovery has been quicker also—after the sedative wears off—he tends to resume a good activity level the day of the shot, which helps mitigate the soreness when that kicks in. So, this has been an area of improvement, though I cannot say we feel more or less committed to the trial. We are scheduled to have an MRI the next time, so we will see what we can gather from that.

Ryland remains status quo, which is great. He continues to revel in his learning and growing. He is physically strong and active, and at this point you cannot see anything wrong really. He does still want Mom, a lot. And he can melt down about seemingly small changes at times. We'll never really know what is normal toddler rigidity or emotional trauma or physical effects in the brain, so it's an evolving parental dance in terms of how much extra leeway to give him vs. firmer limits. But mostly, he is a total joy and so evolved in many ways.

I wish his good functioning could keep our heads out of the abyss more, but the highs are laden with this desperate longing to have them—to have him—forever. And never more so than when I see Ryland and Jane play together, delight in one another, and really get one another. We smile and laugh together a lot, we go along with the kids' discussions about getting older and all the things they envision about that, but as parents we have this horrible secret knowledge about what this diagnosis usually means.

I have been trying to make room in my brain for realism and hope, have tried to broaden my knowledge of health and healing to encompass a spiritual component. I try to hold on to opposites and make them work together somehow, as crazy-making as that can feel sometimes. I would never have chosen to deal with death and dying this directly, but I truly have no choice. It hurts, badly, and we have had some lows here. But that feeling of being gutted sometimes makes room for some unexpected growth. I suspect Ryland will be the greatest teacher I have ever had.

Rigged Game

How can it be that the little boy
Who survived such a calamitous birth
Should so soon be deprived of his life?
Didn't he deserve a better shot?
The long odds that he overcame at the beginning
Are now the infinitesimal and cruel odds
That will likely claim him,
As if at the outset the Bargainer conceded his life
But then changed his mind:
"All right, you may have him,
But only for a little while."
In the face of this terrifying indifference, what?
Only the grace and uncommon substance
Of a dear little boy.
This will be what matters
When the game has played out:
For a time, he has shared his life with us,
Sweetened our world.
Perhaps with this loss then
A great gift,
An opportunity to live life fully with the heart,
As this boy does so well,
So that whenever death comes,
We too will be ready.

April 12...

WE HAD ANOTHER MRI IN PITTSBURGH LAST WEEK. Not a fun morning for Ryland, getting up early, no breakfast, needle into the port (with difficulty), and then two hours on the table under general anesthesia. And that's before the blood draws and injections! (They should seriously give out purple hearts to these kids.)

The main result is that the patch of color that was detected the last time seems to be "evolving": it now looks like a white ring with a darker, necrotic-looking center. As the universe seems to want to continue on the theme of ambiguity, this could either suggest tumor growth or the healing process of a hemorrhage or some kind of radiation or vaccine effect. Other elements of the scan give some hope that it is not tumor, but it's hard to really differentiate between things. Don't get me wrong, I will take ambiguity over certainty that things are heading downhill. It's just frustrating not to have more of a handle on his status, especially as we try to make decisions about his treatment.

Despite these tough trips and the couple days of pain that follow, Ryland's day to day life is still remarkably joyful and healthy. His refrain of "I'm not tired" pretty much sums up his vigor and zest for life. He wants to try new things (hockey is the latest) and he delights so much in the process and the discovery of his abilities. The boy seems active in his sleep, for goodness sake, in all his moving around and desire for cuddles throughout the night (and then up by 5:30!) He still loves to make people laugh, and he likes to get the last laugh, as when he subtly tacks on various potty talk to his "good manners." His loving heart continues to astonish and slay me.

My dad expressed it well, describing Ryland's full embracement of life as making up for time to be lost. That is what it feels like. And likewise, I think I have officially given him enough kisses to fill an average lifespan, with many more on the way.

I continue to seek some solace and the feeling of a bigger picture in the woods behind the house. I have always loved early spring. The warmer sun strikes a marvelous balance with the still cool air. The green of the new vegetation looks almost psychedelic against the brown mud and dead leaves. The singing of birds reassures that I am not just seeing things and that I can trust this miraculous re-emergence of life. I was curious to see if my spring euphoria this year would be seriously dampened by the difficult developments in my life, if the magic would be lost to some sort of cynicism or mistrust in life. I am surprised that this did not happen, considering how nightmarish things have been. I still feel that surge, especially with the opportunity to be outside with the kids and watch them feel it too. And I suppose no matter what happens, I should protect and nurture that joy for life, for that is what Ryland embodies and that is how he chooses to fill his days.

Little Master

Today a friend's kind note steered into view
A beautiful idea.
Her message referenced a Whitman poem
About a young child going forth in the world
And experiencing things in a manner so deep and pure
That those things became part of him…
And he of them,
A lovely and natural symbiosis
"Stretching on forever".
I think of this as Ryland now calls himself
A "big boy"
In a voice that belies his youth,
In a voice that sounds prescient,
In a voice that signals his finiteness.
These days his actions resonate with purpose and conviction,
As if he were making up for time
Soon to be lost,
And so he drinks deeply of his family's love,
Revels in his world with uncommon joy and feeling,
Makes clear to all around him
That this is the way it should be done,
This is how to lead a life…
This, the lesson of our little master.

May 9...

VACCINATION #7 WAS LAST WEEK. No MRI or any clinical changes, so nothing to report on that front. The sedation continues to help with the injections, though he still doesn't like things being done to him medically (understandably)—he fights the numbing lotion at this point. And, as is developmentally appropriate, he shows a good healthy will! If only you could put a toddler's will in pill form you could probably cure just about anything. When he is not resisting, Ryland does often show remarkable patience and adaptability too. He rallies for the flights and meals on the go and whatever sleeping scenario we have planned. Sometimes, when I can block out the whole reason we are traveling, I find these moments of enjoyment just being on an adventure with my son—seeking out a bakery or just taking an urban walk. We are so fortunate he is well enough to do so much.

A few weeks ago I took a hike to the top of that hill where I could view those four trees in their early spring bloom. Three trees had the bright green haze, but the fourth (the one I always thought of as Ryland) looked totally dead. Well, that's f-ing classic I thought, so I ran down the hill to take a closer look. It looked pretty much as lifeless up close. I thought maybe I could see the slightest promising swell of a bud that wanted to emerge, but I couldn't tell if that's what I wanted to see. So I left. A week later I looked up at it from the road below and saw no changes. Then just the other day I went back to the hill, and again saw nothing from the top. So down I went, and lo and behold there were unmistakable leaves shooting out from branches here and there. Not full uniform foliage like the other trees, but life nonetheless. This sight kind of captured the bit of hope we gleaned from a recent conversation with a doctor in Boston to whom we reached out. Though he offered nothing promising in terms of treatment, he believes there is a 1% survival rate, which, after months of hearing "universally fatal" sounds pretty good! Apparently, in rare cases, the tumor just does not grow. So I have been thinking about that and about those late little leaves on the "dead" tree.

I have also been thinking about the limits of strength. Often we think of how "strong" people are when they overcome or endure something. Maybe strength has some role to play in all this, but I think it can be problematic too. It can feel good to be a "strong" parent, carrying on for the kids etc., but when the armor gets too hard the pressure inside has nowhere to go. I feel like it can also promote the kind of thinking that generates this pressure: "if I only love him enough," "if we can figure out just the right plan," etc., etc. The truth is, we do love him to death and there are no right answers and we ultimately cannot control the thing we want to the most. It is scary to surrender to the sheer depths of the emotions that come with this. How can you not drown in that? But it seems like it is better to let those waters rush in sometimes, to allow for chinks and holes and weaknesses, to go to the depths and trust that you will come back to the surface somehow. The times I have experienced this have given me so much more reassurance about life than any attempts at muscling through. It is just counterintuitive when all you want to do is protect yourself and everyone else. Who knew our best protection is in our softest, most human places.

May 13...

THIS MORNING LITTLE RYLAND woke up next to me in bed (where he ends up at some point in the night), looked me in the eyes and said "I love you Mom"—totally unscripted, totally unprompted. Who is this kid? Needless to say, my day was made already. Happy Mother's Day all…

Memorial Day

The signs were there:
The occasional unsteadiness afoot
And bouts of irritability
That were out of character for his sweet self,
So now, making our way through the modest holiday crowd,
We regarded our little boy and his complaining
With more than the usual apprehension
(Days later a scan would confirm our fears.)
We took up position along the parade route,
Parking ourselves in line on a higher than normal curbstone
And so settled, our grandson found his composure
And assumed a centered aspect
That we've seen before,
Uncommon for a child,
Rather the look of a kind old soul about to take
The full measure of the moment.
Without a word, he stood up,
Unwrapped his treat of cornbread,
And proceeded down our line,
Offering what felt like a sacrament
To each one of us in turn.
Speechless like the others,
I had to wonder
Who is this little boy, really,
Who on this day of remembering
Could so stir the soul
Before the first marchers even came into view?

June 5

So, THE MRI LAST WEEK showed a new area of "enhancement," that looks like a white spot of color, surrounded by an area of tumor that appears "bulkier." The other spot we were monitoring before has essentially resolved, and the theory is that it was related to the radiation. We are too far out from radiation to link it to the new spot. The timing now raises the alarm that this could be tumor activity/growth, though the doctor is not ruling out a "vaccine effect" whereby the treatment itself it causing swelling in the area. At this stage it is nearly impossible to differentiate between tumor and treatment. Both could be causing the subtle physical changes we have been worried about lately-mostly some weakness and instability.

Needless to say, it was a difficult trip with an ongoing difficult aftermath for us emotionally. The acute grief and dread and fear all came rushing back in full force. Those feelings have always been around to some degree but his good run had provided flickers of hope. Perhaps we can keep that going and hope this is the vaccine at work, but the brutal truth is that this trial has had no happy endings.

I find myself circling back to feeling of profound injustice with this whole thing. For children to go through this at the dawn of life is so senseless, criminal. When I look at Ryland I see all the promise and potential of an otherwise healthy, happy, loving little boy. He never had a real baby look about him. He has always kind of looked like this handsome little man that you can see at five, at ten, at fifteen, and beyond. I can see his sparkling blue eyes and beautiful smile through all the milestones I long to witness. And yet, microscopic cells have the power to go awry and cause such destruction and suffering. Then I think of all the other remarkable advances and achievements humans have made, and all the other places our resources and energies go in this world...and yet with this, very little progress in thirty years.

There is a place for anger, I know. But it's not a place I feel I can or want to linger. Ultimately love has to be the primary residence: love for him, for my family, for everyone in my life who has enriched it and who have been so generous with their own love and caring.

And when I bemoan the lack of progress, I immediately think of the incredible people working so hard at trying to beat this very challenging disease. We have reached out to physicians in the field, not involved directly in our case, who have been remarkably compassionate and generous with their time. As often in tragedy, the human capacity for good comes shining through, and we are so thankful for that very profound part of this journey.

Granddaughter

A word or two about Jane,
Sweet little Jane, full of wonder,
And remarkably so considering
Hers is a supporting role
In a drama that stars her dying younger brother.

From what five year old depth of character
Has she summoned the equanimity
To minister so keenly to his needs?
When she asks her mother what his death will look like,
Where is that courage coming from?

Oh, she's had her moments,
Anguished tantrums to let us know
That, like any of us caregivers, she needs care as well.
But in all, she has been as stalwart as any adult
And, with her child's insight, able to read her brother's signals
Better than most.

At times she seeks refuge with her alone play
And an array of figurine fairies.
There she stages her own drama
Of hopes and fears
And perhaps happily resolves, in fantastic fashion,
What reality cannot.

Under the most difficult of circumstances,
She bears up well,
But I suspect she'll grow up forever wounded,
Wise before her time,
And likely to acquire, by virtue of a steady flow of caring and sorrow,
A deep wellspring of kindness,
This our sweet Jane, full of wonder.

June 16...

A WEEK AGO, RYLAND was happily engaging in the seemingly benign activity of playing in a tent; however, when stepping out, he fell in an awkward, twisting way to break his femur in his right leg. We had a very painful run over to the ER and then a long wait that evening before he was put under (for the 38th time now) for the bone to be set and for a Spica cast to be put on. We spent a couple nights inpatient to get a better handle on the pain.

We are home now and he is in a cast up to his waist, which will keep him pretty immobilized and in a reclining position for six weeks. The diaper factor has things pretty damp and uncomfortable already—the itch is starting to replace the pain as the main source of discomfort. He is frustrated too about not being able to sit and play with his cars and ride his bike, etc. But his resilience shines through too; he still likes to joke and goof off with Poppi and sing and kiss his mom.

Do I even bother trying to make sense of this? Murphy's Law on steroids? The expression about lightning striking you twice now feels officially inadequate. His increased weakness lately could explain the fall, though he had almost seemed better with that in the days before. We also wonder if the steroids had in fact weakened his bones, though he wasn't on them for a huge length of time. Our oncologist actually normalized the injury in a way—his own son broke his femur at the same age. Toddlers fall, and the femur is susceptible at this age to this kind of spiral break. So perhaps just a little more bad luck...

While in the hospital, we also learned that the Dartmouth team does believe from the latest scans that the tumor is growing, and a subsequent call with Boston rendered the same conclusion. Pittsburgh is sticking with their uncertainty. Tumor progression would mean his time is now limited, though there is variability in terms of time frame. It is possible that he won't be able to walk after the cast comes off. Matt and I find ourselves vacillating between stabbing grief and survival mode where we do just need to get through our days and tend to the kids, which has become much more consuming now with Ryland's needs and Jane's own well-being to protect.

The injury has brought up for us, again, the paradoxes of life. On the one hand, it is the last thing we needed, and this is not how we want him to spend his precious time when his functioning is otherwise good. On the other hand, it feels a bit like a preparation, as grim as that sounds. Instead of a slow robbery of functioning, he has had it taken quickly, and we are all learning how to adjust to a medical situation and how to make his life as good as possible despite the impairments. Matt has also tearfully made the point that right now at least he is here, we are together, we can still make him laugh and love him and he can still be himself.

Back in the fall, someone described to me how shamans often have childhoods in which they experienced significant pain and injury; after being flung against death's door they develop the gift of healing. I found comfort in this and have often called Ryland "my little shaman". Of course, I desperately want him to remain on this side of that door and grow up into the gifted human being I already see. But if he has to go, he will still be my little shaman. His lessons in love and purity and resilience are bigger than death.

Emissary

The day of his birth was auspicious,
A date he shared
With a great grandmother and a great grandfather,
A favorable link to ancestors
So we thought,
And though he himself was born
With neither pulse nor breath,
He was rescued by capable people,
Coming forth as a miracle
And armored, so we thought,
For a long life.

The fatal bit of biology may have been there at the start
Or may have evolved in some unfortunate way,
But far, far too soon after his birth
There it was,
A fatal affront to our expectations.

We have agonized now for some time
Trying to overcome it,
Trying to minimize its symptoms,
Or at least trying to face it
With hope and the best of intentions.

But along the way he has been the one
Doing the real guiding;
He has been the one to show that
Kindness, courage, and love are all that matters
And that together they are an exemplar
Of our best selves.
I suspect his birthday was fateful
And that, connected in a timeless way to his forebears,
He brings us their message.

June 25...

HAPPY BIRTHDAY TO RYLAND! Three years old today. He woke up next to me at the dot of 5:30, the time he was born, in the sweetest of moods. On this day I cannot help but think of his delivery: vivid memories of all that chaos and terror, and ultimately amazement and the height of joy. My little miracle boy. I am glad we didn't know then what more was in store so that we could all treasure the profound relief that he was going to be okay.

Three years later, his birthday brings up the obvious gamut of emotions. But mostly I want to say: Take that, tumor! This is a milestone you cannot claim.

Jane said it the most simply, whispering in my ear: "I'm glad Ryland didn't die before his birthday" (five-year olds are good at cutting to the chase). Yes, we have had to go there with Jane, with the understanding that age appropriate honesty is really the best bet. I can't help but think back to the concern and care that went into trying to prepare her emotionally for a little sibling—that felt like a pretty big deal. It is still surreal to me that I now have to prepare her for something for which I myself will never really be prepared to face. It all can feel a bit above my pay grade (I think I missed this child development class) but all you can do is try to rally and do your best I guess. Thank goodness she is who she is—she seems to be processing it all in a way both tender and strong, thus far anyway. Before the recent conversations, she would often ask: "When I am ten, how old will Ryland be?", "When I am twenty-three, how old will Ryland be?" etc., etc. (a line of questioning a bit painful for the receiver). She hasn't asked those questions lately. The other day in the car she asked: "If Ryland does grow up to be a grownup, who will he marry?"

If I can muster up a fraction of the resilience that my kids have, maybe I will be okay. There are times I feel like the life force is just being wrung from me, often in the morning after a sleepless night when you have to face it all again. But there are wellsprings of fuel around me: the devotion and help from superstar grandparents, a hug from a teacher, a walk with a friend, and of course my little boy rising above everything to smile and to love.

Careful Everyone

No one saw the odd twist and fall of the body
That caused the leg to break,
A plain old fluke perhaps but as likely
Something precipitated by all the earlier steroids
Used to stave off the tumor's symptoms,
Another treatment with a trade-off.

So here we are now, injury added to insult,
And painful irony thrown in for good measure.
What more shall we ask of our young fellow, just turned three?
The ankle-to-waist cast is just the latest challenge,
Causing enough discomfort and irritation after 3 weeks
To send the family back to the hospital.

There in a cheerless little clinic room
A team of doctors set about swapping out the fetid cast
For an improved model,
Something my grandson wanted no part of,
Especially with the unlimbering of a circular saw.

Held down by his parents and other helpers,
He screams heartily enough
That down the hall and through a pair of doors
I can hear him.

What I missed hearing, and reported later,
Was his admonishment to the assembly,
"Be careful everyone!"

For so many days and months prior,
A host of people had, for the most part,
Tried to do that very thing for him,
Through trials and treatments and all manner of medical tribulations,
But even so, he repeated the commandment
That is, after all, our best and basic human charge:
To take care of each other.

His call might also suggest something further:
That we consider leading lives of continuous caring,
That we pay kind attention to calls for help from any quarter,
And that, for at least some moments,
We live thoughtfully outside ourselves.
What better lesson from a mere broken bone?

July 9...

As long as the next X-ray checks out okay, Ryland has just a week and a half left of cast time. He has continued to be a trooper, with remarkable awareness and acceptance of his physical limitations. I have tried to protect him from feeling left out, though yesterday we did bring him to a trip to a lake with Jane and friends—it feels so good to do something normal. Everyone got to take a dip on the warm summer day. Ryland sat contently in his little seat making conversation and requesting snacks. Not a whine or complaint.

The biggest source of discomfort has definitely been the associated skin issues. Suffice to say, I think there is room for some advancements in cast technology, particularly for little ones in diapers. He ended up with a very uncomfortable infection with the first cast (which always seemed to peak in intensity between 10 p.m. and 3 a.m.) that sent us back to the hospital for a whole new cast. This was done in clinic, which meant no sedation of any kind, so we essentially held Ryland down while they sawed off the huge cast (someone also needs to invent a muffler for that saw) and put a whole new one on. He screamed and cried, naturally, and also made an emotional plea to the group of doctors: "Be careful, everyone!" It kills me that there have been so many instances that must have felt like a total assault to him, even if they are efforts to help. It is a miracle, really, that he can reclaim as much calm and trust and good will that he does.

With the new cast (which did include a plastic lining this time) we have seen improvement with the skin issues, thankfully. The positioning of the leg was also changed to the effect that he can better achieve a sitting position and he can also crawl around a bit, dragging the leg behind him. These changes have been huge in terms of what he can do and how he can play. In the last few days he has gotten back on his tricycle for some one-legged peddling and he loves it! It's interesting, these weeks have almost felt like a condensed reenactment of his development: he has learned to roll over, to sit, to crawl, and to play more independently. I suppose next I will be able to see him walk again for the first time.

The cast situation has also given us the experience of having something that we can fix. I think I remember the surgeon saying that the success rate for this was 99 percent—finally, a nice high number working in our favor. When strangers see us out and about and see a toddler in an ankle to waist cast they often give us very sympathetic looks, or say something about it being just the worst thing for a kid this age. Maybe it would have felt that way at one point in our lives.

In terms of the tumor, I can't say I have seen any major neurological changes in the last few weeks. His ability to walk and his balance will be informative. For now though, we are just watching and hoping for continued stability, and we are not actively pursuing medical treatments at this time as there is nothing very compelling out there. We will surely keep our finger on that pulse, though.

I have this medical fantasy (oh how my "happy places" have changed!) that the femur break deactivated the tumor—that because the right side is now compromised, the left side has to be dominant, so the immune system really ramped up to protect the left side against the activity of the tumor. Why not, right?

Birthday Present

My grandson's birthday precedes mine by a week,
So by the time the call came
The old refrain had been well rehearsed:
Over the phone now a gaggle of voices
Singing with gusto
And well out of harmony,
His distinguishable by
An earnest little baritone, unusual for his age.
"Happy birthday dear Poppi, happy birthday to you!"
As joyful a rendition as I'd ever heard,
This was a gift that resonated,
Especially for its little zinger at the end
When some parting endearment was called for
And he chose instead,
 "Please may tootie!"
His contrarian response to requests
For good manners.
So at this milestone at least,
He remains a gremlin after my own heart,
His spirit alive and kicking
And still carrying us along with the mirth
That makes life worth living.

July 19...

Ryland's cast is off. It is amazing, that feeling of flesh and seeing his body again in its unencumbered, unobscured form. No love lost on all that hard scratchy fiberglass. The removal ended up being a little early—Tuesday this week when we were there to see the oncologist for other concerns. Over the weekend he seemed to take a turn: His left side is markedly weaker, speech is a bit slurred at times, and eyes sometime track a little slower. He can't really bear enough weight to crawl, let alone stand or walk. We elected to do a round of Avastin, that may or may not help keep things in check a little, but worth a shot. We have a prescription for steroids which we will use only if it makes the most sense in terms of quality of life (i.e. if his swallowing really starts to go and he still really wants to eat, we hope to find an effective dose to help with that).

So here we are, that dreaded point of disease progression. I knew logically that this was the overwhelmingly likely outcome, though my sense of justice and my hope for my child and my natural feelings as a parent—that he is so exceptional why wouldn't he defy this—have been a wonderful haven against that cruel logic. It is how I have gotten through my days and I don't regret any of it.

Ultimately there is still a place for justice and hope and defiance, but in a different form. We are now charged with guiding him through his final chapter and days, and we will love him and use every strategy we can to make him comfortable and to honor him. I am determined, yes, but truth be known I am also scared and still shocked and so desperately sad. Looking at him today I was again so overwhelmed by his beauty on all levels—how would we begin to live without him? It feels like we are literally being asked to bear the unbearable.

Despite his physical setbacks, Ryland has, if anything, seemed even more lighthearted and tender this week. He is still funny and generous. We have had these lovely bedtimes snuggling in bed and reading...and he will once in a while make eye contact with me and whisper "hi" and "I love you" (which makes my heart explode, and really makes me wonder who is disguised in this three-year-old body).

I have also had powerful exchanges with Jane, often in bed at night or first thing in the morning. She asks about Ryland dying and what that would look like. She told me the other night that she has had "more tears lately" because she "thought she would be able to jump and play and ride bikes" with her brother. Tonight we talked about the ways the tumor can affect the body, and I said something to the effect of loving him for who he is and loving him just as much even if he can't do all the things he used to. Jane said that she in fact "loves him more" and that she "loves him more than the tumor." Hmmm. It seems like if I can give her some simple facts and answers and guidance, she will come back with all the poetry and light. How lucky am I to have her. And him.

W. Horak

Magic Porch

On countless nights we have seen magic from this porch,
Usually on summer's early evenings
When angled light turns green into gold
And swallows gather to perform their aerial wizardry.
This night we saw grace bloom
From desperate soil
And compassion fluoresce
From deepest shadow.
For while the burgeoning tumor in our grandson's brain
Made us tremble
To observe his growing infirmity,
We also witnessed again
The wondrous affection and care
His parents offered in response,
Looks, touches, and embraces
So endearing and deep
That just the memory of them might, in time,
 Heal our wounded hearts
And prove true what Ms. Nye says in her poem,
That kindness is sorrow's sweet offshoot.
So as our miracle boy grows backward
Toward the place before he was born,
We are transfixed by this fleeting moment with its eternal cast:
Him aloft in his father's loving arms
And bathed in the warm, slanting, magical light.

July 29...

WE MADE IT DOWN TO RHODE ISLAND for at least part of a planned trip to the coast. We had a couple alarming episodes with Ryland that sent us home early, but all in all it felt like a victory to get out of the house and plunk his cast-free body in the sand. His several spontaneous declarations of "I love this place" made it feel all the more special.

Of course, the visit stirred up the swirl of mixed emotions I have come to expect from this whole experience. We were thrilled that he was well enough to travel, though seeing him there sort of highlighted his more recent symptoms, as he was in better shape the last time we went. Most obviously, he is unable to walk, and that of course changes things. (I honestly don't know how parents with older and bigger kids do it.) Interestingly, the two times he voiced a desire to walk were the times I felt the sadness of that lost ability the most: first, when we arrived at the house and you want to just all spill out of the car and run on the grass and stretch your legs; and second, when we arrived at the beach and you want to see his feet hit the sand and go. While the sadness lingered for me, Ryland seemed to adapt quite patiently and heroically, sitting in the sand and pushing his trucks back and forth. Certainly, he has his frustrated moments, but overall his ability to adapt continues to amaze and inspire (I think I would have blown a gasket long ago).

There was definitely something nurturing and comforting about being in a place that feels timeless, that hardly changes, that I have known my whole life. There is a feeling of connection to extended family both alive and departed, and the landscape of field and ocean provide a spiritual grounding and sense of awe. Despite these healing properties, however, there is still nowhere to hide from the cutting pain of this threatening loss. To see him on the beach for what will likely be the last time, at three-years-old, was the definition of heartbreak.

One evening we thought he was entering a steep decline. He went to sleep, and we packed up in anticipation of leaving the next day. The grief surged with renewed force, and as I cried in the shower I couldn't recognize my own sobbing—it sounded less personal and more like something ancient or universal. I sat on the porch with Matt and my parents and sister, swollen eyes all around. The sky was filled with threatening storm clouds, of varied formations. The sun set "horizontally" behind a cloud, casting a neon red glow that outlined the dark clouds. It was a strange and captivating sky. But in the immediate surroundings of the house, there was a calm and bright quality to the air, and the swallows performed their swooping show we look forward to each year (they seemed to come a little early). I thought, this is how it is going to go: immense pain, a shattering change, but solace to find in being together.

A big footnote to all this: Since returning home, Ryland has had a pretty stunning rebound. He is crawling around a little more, his eyes appear more normal after some apparent tracking difficulty last week, and he even got on his tricycle and could pedal and hold on. So, the journey continues…

Daughter Again

My daughter says she is more a seeker than a knower
But on the journey we are sharing I think that distinction
May be blurring a bit,
Or maybe it's just that
You can't ever know anything
Without seeking in the first place.
She keeps an open heart and mind,
Records with unflinching attention
Even the most despairing moments along our path,
A first rate journalist of the spirit.
Her words are clear water,
Sustaining, illuminating,
Even as they seep from the deepest layers
 Of pain and anguish.
Along the short track of her son's life,
She has surely come to know pain,
His birth nearly a killer at the outset
And his cancer now a present and consuming peril.
Perhaps his vulnerability has magnified her mother's love,
Forged a bond of infinite caring,
And no doubt provoked her fierce struggle with the question 'why'.
But with few answers in hand
She still seeks hope and promise
Wherever she can,
Believing that if there's any meaning to be had,
It will come only with patient seeking
And a knowing love.

August 14...

Ryland had his third round of Avastin today over at Dartmouth. He handles these hospital trips way better than he should, really. He does not resist going and smiles and jokes with the nurses and doctor. The vital signs are easy now, and today for the first time he did not resist the numbing cream they apply before accessing his port: Seated in his little play car, he very willingly let the nurse do what she needed to do through the car window, and he even helped to raise his shirt. This of course made me lose it, seeing my little boy engaged in his little boy game, stopping to have a numbing agent applied to his port for chemo, as if this is so normal.

The doctor admitted his surprise that Ryland is doing as well as he is. The Avastin appears to have stabilized things for the time being. It essentially blocks blood flow to the tumor. It is not curative, and eventually, resistant tumor cells will overtake the effects of the chemo. But for now I would say his quality of life is pretty good. He is swallowing well enough and communicating. He is able to get around with a sort of "frog hop," bearing weight on both hands and pulling both legs behind in unison (he doesn't really have the bilateral crawl anymore). His left fingers are often fisted, especially when bearing weight, but he can still use the left hand. He does seem weaker in the left leg than two weeks ago; it is a stretch to do even a heavily assisted stand. I do miss seeing him up on his feet.

Ryland remains playful and active. He loves his bike, which we can help push him on, and he often requests to play football and lacrosse in our upstairs hallway. We do these activities from a seated position, of course, and the whole things looks a lot different from the yard play we enjoyed not so long ago. But he still delights in the essence of it: a ball going back and forth between two people with a good amount of "tackling" and kissing thrown in for good measure. When the ball goes past him, he frog hops after it saying, "I can get it!" (Yet another moment that brings tears for me—my tears runneth over!)

While we try to focus on the positives, this has been a very difficult chapter as we basically watch and wait for things to decline. We don't know how long we have, which on the one hand can sharpen our focus on the present moment; but that feeling of dread permeates, and every smile and meeting of eyes twists that knife-edge of loss. When I hold him in bed, it still astounds me that I cannot save him with the sheer size of my love.

Perhaps he will save me with his. When we were down in Rhode Island we had this very memorable exchange one night. He was sitting up in bed, as I was scurrying around getting things ready for sleep time. As I was exiting into the bathroom, he says, "Mom, I love you." I turn and take a step towards him and say I love him too. Then he brings his finger to his lips which were parted into a little smile and says, "Shhhhh, I love you", and repeats that a couple times, looking deeply into my eyes. It brought me to a complete stop. It reminded me of my friend Karen's words about slowing down, and about absorbing his love into every cell. I've never been so good at "slow" let alone "stop" but leave it to Ryland to show me the way, and the why.

Knife Edge

A child's life hangs in a balance
And the wait may not be worth it,
Our only gratification may just be in the delay.

The days have become a continuous negotiation
Between hope and despair,
Joy and pain,
Laughter and suffering,
Between whatever the hell you care to imagine
Defining life's extremities.

For stretches of time one holds forth over the other,
Dominates your point of view,
But with one small flicker of feeling
The roles reverse,
The opposite takes hold,
And so the exchange continues.

It is a duality that in effect produces another:
An exhaustion that weighs so heavily on the spirit
That finding a hole and crawling in
Is your best option,
A mighty relief from the burden.

At the same time comes a sharpening of focus,
A level of attention that feels new,
Things perceived clearly for the first time,
Blinders off once and for all.

Walking sharply down that middle path,
Opening up to the extremities on either side,
Is what I've come to understand as necessary;
But truth be told,
I'd abandon this knife-edge of understanding
And, in a heartbeat, embrace the dullness of a former ignorance
In exchange for my grandson's life.

August 31

RYLAND HAS SHOWN A SHARP DECLINE THIS WEEK. Eating, drinking, and even communicating have become more difficult. With the swallowing reflex compromised, he drools almost constantly and coughs a lot to clear his lungs. His head tilts to the left, and he is generally quite a bit more weak. He can still scoot around a little when energized, but at times needs support to sit. Our care has been transitioned to the palliative team and hospice at this point.

This decline followed a wonderful series of get-togethers with friends on beautiful summer nights, in which his spirit shined through all deficits. Even now, he is generous with his smile, and notably social and emotionally connected to the people in his life. He requests different people to do different things for him, in a way that spreads his love around and includes everyone in his life.

At the same time, he becomes tearful more often, and I am sure he is struggling with the deterioration of his functioning. We are trying to alleviate this in whatever ways we can.

This is also the week Jane started kindergarten, so I am watching one child take a big exciting step into her future, while I watch the other go in reverse. I'm not sure I can fully comment on that experience yet; I just have a feeling that I will be processing this week for a long time. I can say that Jane seems to be doing very well. She has embraced this change with joy and confidence, and I am just so proud of her and excited for her.

And concurrent with those feeling are the devastation, the anxiety, and also the determination to do what is right for Ryland. It is a stare down with my deepest darkest fear, and I cannot turn away. Whatever this does to me, I do know this is the hardest and most important work I will do, not by choice but by assignment. And as I take these steps into the dark, into this nightmare from which I still want to awaken so badly, I think of that net of people in my life who could shorten the fall and cushion the blows. Thank you to everyone who continues to walk this walk with us through your thoughts, prayers, notes and just plain willingness to be "with" us. I can attest to the power of that.

Boat trip

Today I encountered him at mid-voyage
Swaying unsteadily on all fours,
A compromised engine
Pushing a favorite toy boat across the floor.
Perched on a threshold, he was headed from his play area
To the distant shore of Nonni's and Poppi's room
Many leagues away across the living room.
And no amount of drool, or snot, or bodily infirmity—
None of these insulting affronts
To his doughty spirit—
Would get in the way.
At three years young,
He has always been the captain of his soul,
A person of strong conviction,
Even now as the disease assaults every aspect of his being.
It was an obvious, but still touching metaphor, this trip,
And complete it he did,
To our room and back.
In so doing, I was reminded again
Of how inspired any journey may be,
Even when time is short,
Even when the flesh is weak,
But invariably, only when the aim is true.

September 6...

I WAS TALKING WITH A DEAR FRIEND THE OTHER DAY ABOUT ANGER, and to what extent this comes up for me. Oddly, it hasn't been a strong emotion as of yet, and I wonder if it is building somewhere that I don't have access to. Mostly I just think that the sadness is so profound that it just dominates, and I also think that anger is often just a cover for sadness and hurt anyway.

But I will say that something akin to anger has been coursing through my body as I watch Ryland lose his ability to speak. It has been torturous enough to watch his mobility go but to watch him now struggle to express himself feels especially appalling. There is something most precious about the sound of your child's voice (and so particularly cute at three), not to mention all the vocabulary he has built and all the humor and love he expresses verbally. Fortunately, my mommy ears are still pretty well honed, so that I can decipher most things he says. To someone else something might sound like spit mixed with a few vowels, but I can somehow get: Oh you want to have applesauce and then go find your tractor! When it works, I feel like I have a super power. But I know it won't always work, and I dread the day, for as a mother you are hardwired to understand and meet the need.

This is a cruel disease. Since birth we have cheered for his every advancement and milestone. In this way I feel like we encouraged him to trust life, to trust his future would be there for him, and this illness and what it does to the body can feel like the most horrifying breach of trust. But beyond the tumor cells I can't even see, there is no one to blame, no apparent environmental demon to rage against. For me, "fairness" doesn't come up as a concept here because it would imply that someone else is more deserving of this fate, and that is simply not in my heart. So we are left with the age-old lesson that suffering happens, and that we have such limited control. It still feels damn unjust for an innocent child.

I know bereaved parents who have channeled this feeling into efforts to fight the disease and find a cure. There are inspirational foundations out there raising money toward research, and Matt and I are considering doing something in honor of Ryland. We will let you know. In the meantime, we deeply appreciate the growing participation in the CHaD (Children's Hospital at Dartmouth) Half Marathon this October, either through running/walking or donating. The collective spirit and effort feel like a very powerful counter punch to the blow we have sustained. (Hmm, maybe there is some anger there if I'm talking about punching...)

Gestures

You could easily miss them
Because he is still so small
And because the disease has now sapped
So drastically his body and his voice,
But there it was the other early morning,
His feeble hand extended to his sister
With a spoonful of breakfast
And a slurred, barely decipherable,
"Want some, Jane?"
I ask myself:
What child spirit makes such a gesture,
Even now from the far edge of his own life?
Somehow he knows,
Somehow he knows,
Somehow he knows
That kindness is the way.

September 11

WE HAD, WHAT WAS LIKELY, our last appointment over at Dartmouth today. Ryland is at a point now that hospice in the home is all that really makes sense. So, we had emotional goodbyes with our team there.

It was one year ago today that we brought him to Dartmouth with concerns over his left hand and slight limp. In the wee hours of the morning, he would be put under for his MRI, and by 3 a.m. we would know the diagnosis that would change our lives so violently and suddenly. The images will forever be vivid: the long white corridor and the black night out the windows; the empty, sterile waiting room where we waited for over two hours, with the growing sense of foreboding. Then it was like a free fall into an abyss of pain that seems to have no bottom.

The year brought many insane chapters and decisions. It also included hope and love and the deep comfort of family and community.

Four seasons have passed, and nature has been both a source of grounding as well as a sort of mirror of our experience. From the top of a hill the other day, I felt how summer has been holding on extra-long this year, with the warm days and the lingering green all around. But there is an unmistakable feeling of change in the air: You can tell that the mountains will soon be ablaze and that the chill will set in more permanently. So it is with Ryland. He continues to smile and charm; he continues to move himself around with two fisted hands, on his knuckles like some little marine; and he continues to enjoy his meals, even if it literally takes hours to do the work of chewing and swallowing. But you can feel in his weakening that our time together is winding down.

I saw four bears on four different walks in the woods this summer. It became a little bit of a joke how this kept happening (my mom is still trying to find the humor in it I think). Truthfully, these encounters were far more awe than fear inspiring. That feeling of being "in nature" deepens so much when you are in the presence of something so wild and powerful, and when your own animal nature becomes more activated. A friend of mine recently illuminated some symbolic associations with the bear, and clearly the maternal and protective resonate with me. I just hope to have an ounce of that power, after the worst powerlessness I have ever known.

I will need it as we approach these coming days/weeks, uncertain of how things will unfold exactly, hoping for whatever biological mercy can be rendered by the way the tumor grows and takes functions. We do not want him to suffer or to be afraid, and we know medicine can help with this. Right now, we continue to follow his lead...

Gaze

He can do so little these days
And without his voice, we depend on just little signs,
Little looks to clue us in.

A barely perceptible headshake and a grimace
Tell us no more Jell-O, thank you,
While a lip-curled smile á la Elvis
Means he liked the joke.

Tonight though, he floats in a bath,
Face up, loose-limbed, buoyed by his mother,
Sliding him on tender hands,
Gently, gently back and forth,
A fluid motion that might well be
Summoning his amniotic past.

Back then they were bound together in one form,
But here now, eyes locked on each other's
They seem no less so.

His blissful gaze comes up from a deep faraway place,
A reservoir of boundless trust and gratitude
Where cancer may make no inroad,
Pain left far behind.

Her downward look mirrors his,
A beam of devotion
Breathtakingly personal and universal
In the same instant,
A mother loving in the absolute manner of all mothers.

Here on this journey, another timeless moment:
A gaze that tells us that
They have likely loved
In some lifetime before
And are surely to again in another,
Drifting, drifting together in gentle water.

September 23...

RYLAND CONTINUES TO SOLDIER ON, as his body continues to go in reverse. He can no longer support himself with his arms, so we are mostly holding him. He has also lost most head and neck control, so we support his head like a little baby, albeit with more difficulty at his size. He has lost all language, so we are back to trying to read his physical cues and make best guesses as to his needs. We have baby food in the house again, which he can get down with some effort, along with yogurt and Jell-O for hydration. Like in infancy, we find ourselves preoccupied with poops again, as those systems are not working like they used to.

He has also developed a strong liking for the bath, and as I lay him back in the warm water and observe the instant calm and pleasure in his face, I feel like I am seeing him back in the womb. Despite all of these changes and regressions, he is still Ryland. This tumor does not take intellectual function, so I know there is still so much going on inside. He will still give a recognizable chuckle to something humorous, and when given the chance and the audience he will still try to exercise his inner rascal, in whatever way he can. He is still very much connected to the people in his life.

For the parents, it continues to be a life of utmost vulnerability and despair, coupled with the need to function and be strong all at the same time. The grandparents, no doubt going through a very similar psychology, have continued to come through with boundless support. Again, like after the arrival of a new baby, but now in preparation for something much different.

Many have asked what they can do, and while a lot of the concrete things along the way have been so helpful, there isn't a whole lot of that to be done now. Matt described it best recently: When someone offered to "do something," he wanted to reply, "You just did." The simple caring and willingness to be with us emotionally are perhaps the most powerful things. And no one has to feel the need to "be strong" for us either; if tears come, you are simply speaking our language!

That emotion is the definition of compassion, and that is what gets us all through at the end of the day.

September 29...

NOT SO LONG AGO, I was able to look at old photographs or videos of Ryland. Right now, I notice that I am unable to. When I see old footage of a healthy, vibrant boy, I see all that has been taken from him in a way that is too shocking and difficult, even if I have lived through every single loss already. Somehow, many of his prior functions already feel incredibly distant: his ability to walk, his ability to feed himself, even the sound of his speech.

I don't want to feel those losses right now. I don't want to feel a longing for another time. All I want is to love Ryland for who is he right in this moment, and the truth is he is still my perfect baby, even with those crossing eyes and rigid limbs and drooling mouth. He is still the most beautiful being, and I want him to know that and to know my unconditional love as deeply as possible. In my time with him now, I find that I am not as sad or tearful, even though his death feels more certain and soon than ever before. Right now, as I cradle him and we look deeply into each other, I simply feel connection and love in the purest form I have known. No projections, no dreams for his future, no pride in accomplishments or talents, no distractions…

Someday I will treasure all the pictures; someday maybe it will be possible to integrate everything that has happened into some sort of whole. But for now it is true that the moment is all there is.

October 14...

HERE WE REMAIN IN THIS END PHASE, which had sounded so completely terrifying in our research a year ago. It is still difficult, no doubt, though perhaps that terrifying quality has dissipated in some strange way. I guess once the anticipation is over and you actually have to march on through the things that were so fearful, you find there is no room for the fear itself. A prime example would be the deterioration of Ryland's vision in recent weeks; though I feel like he can see something, perhaps shape or color, he tends to nod "no" when asked if he can see things. I knew this tumor could take vision, and that had felt like a complete nightmare. But now what can we do but adapt and carry on. And once again, it is his bravery and patience with it all that remain the greatest inspiration.

Who knows, perhaps I am so just entrenched in the caretaking that the fear and other strong emotions have been naturally buried for the time being. He is in our arms for pretty much the entire day, and we are constantly trying to read his body language and symptoms to assess his comfort and intervene appropriately. Thankfully he can still nod yes and no to our questions, and with the yeses he often adds blinking for emphasis, with those impossibly long and beautiful lashes of his. While I feel like we are doing the best we can, his comfort is still more of a moving target than I would like it to be, and at times it can be difficult to differentiate between frustration and physical issues.

Incredibly, he is still swallowing enough Jell-O to hydrate and can get down a few other soft foods (yogurt, pudding). The method may appear a bit crazy: I basically have to hold him horizontally and drop the food in between a narrowing gap in his teeth. A normal person would gag, but he has figured out that this is the way he can continue to "eat and drink." Things will go down the wrong way at times, but after some rattling he can still clear his lungs well enough.

He is weaker overall, but I wouldn't necessarily say "less alert" at this point. He continues to fight sleep the way he always did (though will sleep a decent amount eventually). He also has enough of a rascal spirit to devise and partake in a joke he is physically able to play: After convincing me it's time to change the diaper, he will take advantage of a bare moment to pee all over, the delight of any normal boy I suppose! The right side of his mouth will curl into a little smile and some twinkle will return to the eyes—a result that has me indulging the game as often as he wants and welcoming the added laundry.

Honestly, I did not think he would still be with us around the time of the CHaD event. But here he is plugging along, not without difficulty but still with humor and resilience. I cannot predict where we'll be a week from now, but if we can make it to Hanover next Sunday we will. (And how about the Run4Ryland team being in the top spot right now! Go team, and thank you!)

I will close with Jane, a guiding light for us like her brother. First of all, she appears to have found a beautiful balance between engaging in her own life and activities and also very genuinely tending to her brother on an emotional level. She protects his feelings by being subtle about special foods he cannot have and activities he cannot do. At times she will naturally go to his side to entertain him, when I need to step away for a moment. She will make him cards with messages that reflect a grasp of his reality ("Dear Ryland, have a great day napping and sleeping and snuggling with Mom.")

And then, the other day, out of the blue, she stated to me that, "Dying will be much easier than having the tumor." She listed off all the hardships in thoughtful detail (not being able to talk, problems with vision, etc.) and then said, "When you die you just"—and she acted out closing her eyes and sort of leaning over. I really don't think I gave her this idea... it seemed to come from some intuitive place in herself. And what a gift to us, as we anticipate the end and work so hard to support his quality of life right now, to be reminded of the freedom and peace that await him.

Dance

This cruel disease now metes out
The worst sorts of indignities.
Robbery of voice, sight, movement,
Even his ability to swallow.
To the uninitiated it appears
Horrifying, unbearable.
And yet, and yet,
His loved ones know
What keen spirit lies within,
A bright mind ticking smartly
Inside the hopelessly damaged shell.
With that, the exquisite dance between them can continue.
He gives tiny signals to direct the care giving:
Eyelid flutter an assent,
Slight back-and-forth of the head a no,
The quiver of the index finger for something else.
The little moves made together are now triumphs,
Jell-O swallowed, baths taken, books read and understood.
There'll soon come a time of course
When the dancing does stop,
When he retreats farther down and away
To a place of only silent knowing…
Before he leaves for good.
But until then, they take their delicate steps
Together.

October 17...

It was as if Ryland was holding on strong for my birthday on Monday, as he has declined significantly since then. Today was the first day he did not take any fluid; his breathing is more erratic and rattling with fluid, and he is weaker and limper. We are doing regular doses of morphine now. He is still able to open his eyes and do his little nods. And though some weight loss is starting to become apparent, he in many ways still looks like a glorious physical specimen with those broad shoulder and big barrel chest like Daddy's.

As I write, both kids are in our bed upstairs (where we will all sleep together now) and Jane is singing songs to her brother all on her own.

I was talking with a friend last night about how, with this disease, you just seem to keep hitting new bottoms over its course. Just when you acclimate (sort of) to a new reality of bodily dysfunction, the tumor proceeds to take more. And when that happens, whatever psychic dam had formed to somewhat contain the waters of grief gives way and you are flooded in a way that feels choking. And eventually you do come up for air, but there just seems less to be had now.

So I don't know if our little hero will make it on Sunday, but we will still shoot for an appearance on Saturday at the potluck.

I did my usual hike to the look out to check on my trees. The backdrop was a wash of autumn color that felt very muted this year, maybe even somber, but that could be in the eye of the beholder. Anyway, there was the little "Ryland" tree, pretty much bare, with maybe one little leaf on it (the three others had quite a few more leaves). A sad sight maybe, but I couldn't help but think how the tree had sprung to life this year, from seeming decay. And I did think of Ryland's year, and the many joys amidst the struggles.

And one more story. Matt and I went to the cemetery this morning to claim Ryland's "lot," so that we know where he will be. One can probably imagine our emotional state. Anyway, we approach the general area we are considering and an older man on a lawn tractor pulls up and stops. We've never met—he has no idea who we are and why we're there. The first thing he says is: "So I saw a bear come through here yesterday!" and proceeds to tell us about the deer that also frequent the place. He points out his own gravestone already in the ground, with a bear and a deer etched in the stone on either side of his name.

The bear thing again. In this crushing and absurd trip to find a resting place for our beloved three-year-old boy, I feel like I had a little wink from the universe that maybe things make more sense than I know. Please let it be so…

Suspension

Caught in a tortuous limbo,
Dangling somewhere
Between hope and oblivion,
Grateful for each day
But desperate that each day passing
Brings us closer
To a terrible end point.
How to manage this?
How to live with this?
I pay attention and am uplifted by signs,
Some as miraculous as the butterfly
Alighting on my shirt the other day,
But tormented by others
As mundane and dreadful as the dead flies
I sweep up in the dustpan.
This is hard business
This life and death business,

But I would have preferred another messenger,
Someone other than a child
To bring it to mind.
If I had paid better attention,
Might that have changed things?
Might that have spared a life?
But this is selfish thinking
For now I am suspended, waiting.

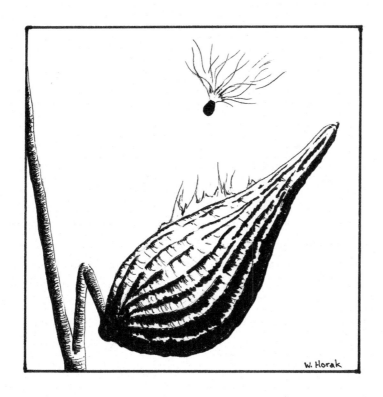

October 22...

RYLAND DIED IN MY ARMS TODAY, October 22, around 1:15p.m. Matt was right there too, huddled in close, and we whispered our final "I love yous" and caressed him as he took his last breaths. Ryland's Nonni, Poppi, Grandma, and friend Richard were close by in the adjoining room.

He had spent a quiet and peaceful morning in the arms of family.

Matt and I took separate walks this morning to the same place, and both had similar experiences. It was a beautiful day, warm and windy, mostly sunny with striking clouds traversing the sky. As I stood atop the hill, I watched a milkweed seed (the kind with the white fluff that Jane calls "fairies") blow across the hill below, heading for the woods. At the edge of the woods, a different current of air reversed its direction and then took it sailing up and out into the sky. I watched, expecting to lose sight of it any second, but then it changed course again and started coming straight back towards me. I kept watching it, but then strangely, as it drew closer, it seemed to disappear, into the heavens.

Matt described a very similar sight of a milkweed "fairy" vanishing, slipping into another realm. He also observed how the wind today seemed to turn fall upside down by sending leaves aloft into the sky.

Despite our anguish, I cannot think of a better send-off for our precious boy. The CHaD Run/ Walk was yesterday and though he could not make it, Ryland was aware of the outpouring of love and support happening close by. He was the runner of his own race, and he made it to race day.

And then today had a palpable feeling of calm. He had intimate time with family, and then waited to be in my arms before letting go. I was not able to hold Ryland right after he was born, but today I had the honor of holding him close as he made this transition. Jane had time with him too today. She wept and snuggled his little body and was herself enveloped by all of her loving family.

We are grateful to our entire community of friends and family, near and far, who have given us love and strength.

We are grateful to Ryland, who has embodied love and strength, and who has taught us so much. We hope you are running free somewhere with the wind at your back. We love you forever and ever.

Departure

It's hard to think, let alone write
Through this thick slop of pain,
But after all, after everything, Ryland warrants the testimony.

He died some days ago in his parents' loving arms,
And while we had long anticipated that moment,
His last breath provoked from us
A chorus of wails and gasps
That seemed to come from an ancient and
Nearly unrecognizable place within.

Even though his wasted frame
Might have had us welcome death for its surcease,
Our hearts cried otherwise,
And in the ensuing minutes and hours
We rode alternating waves
Of panic and shock and despair,
Until small pieces of grace mercifully floated through,
Each of us summoning up little kindnesses
That, after all, were his trademark.
And so we honored him with an afternoon
Of looks, touches, and embraces
Of the most loving and primal kind.

Lying in bed for that protracted time, he aged before our eyes,
And it seemed that with each embrace
We could see by increment more of the old soul
We all along suspected him to be.

His child's flesh gone lean and taut and solemn,
He had taken on the mien
Of the man we would never know in this life,
And so his death was also a revelation.

At nightfall Ryland left us,
Carried out the door in the arms of his mother
And with our entourage that cohered around them
Spontaneously, instinctively,
Bearing collective witness
To a departure unrehearsed, authentic, grave:
A passage then from mother's arms to father's arms to gurney,
The moments tender and torturous,
And all of us struggling to trust in the mystery of it all.

Placed uncovered in the vehicle, his body had a glowing pallor
That allowed us to track his leaving down the darkened lane.
As he always insisted, as he would have wanted,
A few last loud beeps of the horn,
And he was gone.

Loss

Lodger

Sorrow came to my door
And let himself in,
An uninvited guest
Soon become a permanent lodger.
I have no choice in the matter,
Only to sit and listen
To what he has to say.

October 25...

JANE'S LITTLE REFRAIN THIS WEEK helps to describe where we all are: "I can believe Ryland is gone and I can't believe Ryland is gone." A year of anticipation, grief, and "preparation" and yet you are never fully prepared to be on this side of things. I still have this feeling like we are not built to do this, that this is brutally unnatural. But still you have to walk through it, with the hope that the brutality will evolve into something at least a bit easier to carry. To say I miss Ryland captures nothing...I ache for him from the bottom of my being. And time and the mind do curious things. I not only expect (want?) to see him resting in bed...my ears are still tuned into his little footsteps, and my eyes search for the busy body and radiant smile of his healthy days. We are not the first or last parents to lose a child...I just still cannot believe that this happens to people. All I can think of is—we have to stick together as human beings to be able to bear life's sufferings.

Attachment

Now I fully understand that we love at our own peril,
Become forever vulnerable
When we attach our hearts.

Once we do, never imagining life
Without the attachment,
Depending on it, needing it,
As much as air and water.

The peril deepens with the enterprise of children and family,
As expectation and hope cohere with love,
These accruing inevitably with offspring,

As if progeny were the hope of the world
Or perhaps just the fulfillment of our own unfinished business.

Children, grandchildren: iterations of ourselves,
Extensions of life, offering us second and third lifetimes,
And so we love them madly and deeply beyond measure.

To lose them produces pain
In exact inverse proportion:
Grief and despair beyond measure,
A wounding beyond description,
Brought forth by a brutal disruption of a natural order:
Parent outliving a child.
But none of this is new, the love and loss,
And as searing and fresh as the pain now feels,
It is ancient and endlessly repeating…
Welcome, finally, to the human family.

Pain, the payment due for the love engaged,
No love story without an end, in the end always a loss.
As Buddhists would have it,
We need to open our hearts
To this inevitability and to its corollary:
That our children were never ours exclusively,
Their fate never ours to administer.

So I need to welcome pain as a necessary guest,
A teacher to remind me to loosen attachments,
To lose them utterly
And even to let my grandson go
In a manner beyond imagining.

November 18...

It has been two weeks since Ryland's service and nearly a month since he died. I feel like I am living on another planet where time has lost all linear shape; it feels like an eternity since I last held him, and yet the images of his dying moments are as vivid as yesterday. And my overwhelming love and grief are forever present.

My prior feelings remain true, that even with significant time to "prepare" for Ryland's death, I feel like I am starting from scratch. There is a giant gulf between caring intensely for an ill child and then existing in the world without him. There is "anticipatory grief," but then the real grief is its own animal. I am at the beginning of a process that has no end, and I don't feel like much of an active agent in it all. I can take care of myself, I can accept help, but mostly it seems like grief is going to be something that happens to me, in whatever rhythm and flow it wants. I can anticipate and get used to certain jolts, whether from the car seat I cannot take out of the car or the toddler spoons we keep in the drawer, but there will probably forever be moments or memories that catch me off guard and bring the tears no matter where I am or what I'm doing. The mundane task of getting the humidifiers out for winter prompted an unexpected deluge—what to do with Ryland's duck?

I will say that the memory of his service will always bring comfort, as I think of that love-filled space and moment. Thank you to all who contributed their love that day, whether inside the chapel or from afar.

I also wanted to thank everyone who has followed his story here. What started as a place for information sharing became an important opportunity to try to capture the emotional journey and also document my child's life—the tumor could take everything, but not his story. This also became such a meaningful and healing dialogue with a beautiful spectrum of loved ones in my life. I appreciate the encouragement to write. I probably shouldn't stop now, even if general motivation is in the tank much of the time. But I will try, if not here then somewhere.

With gratitude to all this week of Thanksgiving.

January 13...

I HAVE NOT REALLY BEEN ABLE to write—mostly I am just sort of mucking through what my dad so aptly describes as a "thick slop of pain." A wise woman who lost a child told me that my job this first year is just to survive, and I am taking her counsel to heart. I am moving slowly though the slop. While Ryland is literally present in my mind at all times, I sometimes feel like a certain numbing occurs. It can feel like a double life sometimes, not in the sense that I feel like I have to hide or deny my pain, but just that sometimes I need to be and want to be more functional. And there are plenty of "trapdoors" to bring me right back down to the fuller force of the grief.

Jane has had her own ebbs and flows. She enjoys school and her activities, but at times it is hard for her to transition back to home where she still feels his absence so acutely. She is trying hard to adapt, but it is simply not the same without her playmate, and she will cry in her longing for him. As hard as it is to see, I am in the end grateful that she is as expressive as she is, and somehow finding her own balance between functioning and grieving.

The other major development, which I will make official here, is that we are expecting a child this summer. I don't think I'll even try to articulate what kind of a mind-bender that is, but it is a good thing. Words like "excited" don't really work anymore—there is a bit of a lost innocence with the whole thing to be honest. But still, it is good. The due date is just about a week off from Ryland's birthday. The growth rate of this one seems to be happening in direct defiance with the emptiness I feel—I'm not sure how my body is holding death and life all in the same space. In her animated way when she has a realization, Jane one day said: "Mom! You know, kids can be in three different places, the spirit world, our world, and a mommy's tummy, and you have all three!" I guess she's right…

Here's to some positive developments in the New Year.

Dare

Ryland will have a younger sibling,
A fact that left us speechless upon the announcement
And that now requires the heart to perform
The ultimate trick of holding
Sorrow and joy together, beat by beat by beat.

This daughter of mine carries off the feat
On a daily basis, for all to see,
No sleight of hand or mind necessary,
But I cannot fathom how she does it,
How she nurtures new life
While grieving beyond measure
The young life lost to her.

The two are connected in some powerful,
As yet dimly understood way,
But if there's some understanding to be had,
My daughter will find it.

Her honesty must be the source of the magic,
The grace that saves her (and the rest of us),
Even as she acknowledges the fickle nature
Of cells dividing,
Holding such promise with one,
Exacting such cruelty on the other.

She risks it all again, doubling down on her loss
For the sake of a new life,
For the sake of her loved ones,
For Ryland and all who hold him close in their memory.
It is a brave thing to want to love that deeply again,
But, following her lead, we all take up the dare.

January 23...

IT HAS BEEN THREE MONTHS SINCE RYLAND DIED. It was like grief's first trimester (of infinite trimesters), a time when my energies spiraled inward as if into a vacuum of boundless sorrow, when the sheer weight of the loss felt paralyzing. Ironically of course, I was also in my first trimester of pregnancy. A loss of life and a beginning of life happening simultaneously, so that I couldn't tell one hormone from the next or know which was making me feel more ill or drained. It doesn't matter. I knew I just had to surrender to the feelings, to move slowly, to conserve my energy.

Three months out the pain is no less, but there is an emerging impulse to do something with it and a feeling that it needs to move. So I will finally put it on the page, in real time, without knowing where this might go. It is not an attempt to exorcise the grief or even lessen it in any real way. I know it will always be there, self-generating no matter how many tears fall. But it needs to flow in some way, like the tears. And maybe there are things to capture about it, maybe it is a living outgrowth of Ryland's life and my love for him that would be a shame to lose too.

My first question is: What is the nature of healing from a wound that can never fully close? Perhaps you can stop the major bleeding, numb it when necessary. But any suture will surely tear at the force, and then what? I suspect it will simply remain there to tend, to blot, to disinfect, to grin and bear when life demands other things of you, but also to protect and honor. How do you move through life, with this pain now a constant? I suspect you try to make your moves wisely, to rein in your life in some ways to conserve your resources, but to expand it in other ways to enhance those resources. I make these guesses based on my experience so far, but there is also an unknown about the future that I have come to accept.

A loss of a child is bigger than anything I have ever known, other than perhaps the love of a child. My life is no longer what it was—it died with him—and I cannot pretend to wrap my head around that change right now and to fully imagine what this new life might be. Right now, I am becoming acquainted with the wound that I will carry—to imagine eating my next meal with it, picking my daughter up from school with it, going to sleep at night with it. This grief work is my life's work, which I did not choose but that I cannot ignore. There will be no path to follow this time, no educational degrees or other such markers. It's more like bushwhacking without a map, and if that is outside any sort of comfort zone then I suppose that is the whole point! But I will find you, my love, with machete in hand, sweating and bleeding and driven by the purest of devotion.

No Normal

There is no normal,
Or the true normal is something other
Than what I'd been told.
All those expectations and assumptions
About what life might reasonably look like
Are gone
Like an exhalation in a windstorm.
The cultural paradigms that link
Hard work and good intentions
To success and happiness
Are only advertisements after all,
And the truth lies elsewhere
In the age-old narratives that tell
Of hardship and loss.
My own sweet family now thrown over
By a pernicious disease,
I rail at my particular misfortune,
Only to hear, finally, all the voices
Of so many other afflicted souls
Who left normal long ago.
I feel welcome in their ranks,
If not relieved, at least comforted to understand
That life does go on,
Shattered heart and all.
This now is my normal,
This is where I belong.

January 29...

WHERE ARE YOU NOW, RYLAND? For over three years I knew exactly where you were at any given minute. For much of that, you were in my arms. How can you possibly be gone so completely, so suddenly? Your pictures, which I want to treasure, seem to only taunt me right now with their detail and two-dimensional form. Yours was a face I could not stop staring at, and now quite cruelly yours is an image that is difficult to bear. It says: Look what you had and look what you lost.

Are you in another realm? Can you see me? I am lacking in certainties about death and what comes next. I had reached a sort of peace with these unknowns, but your departure brings more urgency to the search. I have been learning about theories of eternal consciousness, which are so compelling and appealing. But certainty does not come easily to me, and my search for you must be the truest thing I have ever done, as true as my love. Perhaps my whole life will be a journey to find you.

Many say that you will live in my heart and memory. Yes, it seems you must be woven into my being somehow, the way you have a constant presence. The more specific memories are more difficult, like the pictures in how they accentuate what has been taken. Memories have more sweetness when you still have more to make together. And what about the body? The love of a child has such a physical dimension. Was there anything better than holding you, squeezing you, kissing you? Everything about the body was pleasing: your toes, your thighs, your tummy, your breathtaking face, your tousled blond hair. We parents are built to feel no greater affection and protection than that for our small children; it is so deep it is almost painful. So how to let that go, even with a promise that you will live on in a spiritual and emotional sense.

And of course, beyond the body, there was you. There is only one Ryland, with your signature wit and wisdom, honesty and tenderness, intelligence and playfulness. Were your gifts meant to be temporary, despite my maternal projections about where they might take you as a grown man? Were you in fact the old soul you appeared to be all along, only needing a short time here to evolve and inspire? This may be so, but I would much prefer for your gifts to be lived out here, with us, as son, brother, grandchild, nephew, friend. Does the world not need that kind of joy and camaraderie and love of a family, whole and intact? We want to find meaning for our losses and our suffering to make them more bearable, and I have been able to do that fairly well until now. But sometimes you have to sit with the pure tragedy of an event, without a rush to understand. And so I sit, missing your body and your dazzling little self; missing the source of my pride and my sense of meaning in the world (which, of course, Jane continues to give in her own way). And still wanting to check on you and make sure you are okay. I will never stop looking for you.

February 2...

It is February, usually that time when winter starts to feel long and I start feeling itchy for spring. Spring is usually a time of euphoria for me, with its thaw and rebirth and transformation of the landscape. What about this year? More than ever, winter fits my mood, mirrors my own inner landscape. Ryland's death towards the end of October ushered in the season of winter so perfectly: The last bits of color faded into November gray, the last gusts of warmth gave way to cold. I have wanted nothing more than to hole up, and the hibernation instincts of winter and of grief work together. There has been an end of life inside the home and out, and there is almost something comforting in the synchronicity of that.

I feel somewhat anxious about spring: What will the relationship to that season be now? There is a catch-22 in the making. Not to welcome that euphoria would be sad, but then again how does that emotion co-exist with the depth of my longing and grief? Or maybe the human heart is capable of both, without tremendous angst and dissonance. As with so many things, the answer to the how may only come from the doing, which will be inevitable with the passage of time.

This challenge with the seasons may inform how I welcome a new life into our family amidst all the sorrow and pain. I am about half way, with the baby due shortly after Ryland's own birthday, June 25. This pregnancy is interesting; the growth of my belly seems very strong and steady, like an assurance that this is in fact happening, and yet this baby seems quiet and mellow in terms of movement, as if it doesn't want to impose its presence too much. I am feeling ready for more movement though, for signs of robustness and health. I am feeling ready to connect, despite my yearning to be with Ryland; I don't want one to crowd out the other. Ryland and the baby will show me how, as my rational adult mind struggles with the riddle. No emotion can be forced, only recognized and nurtured as it evolves from a deeper and authentic place. This is after all what Ryland demonstrated so beautifully: an honesty and purity in his feelings and actions.

Thanks goodness for February, then, the month that always gave me the most trouble. Because I still want to hole up a bit, and feel like nature understands my pain and can describe how bleak I feel when words fail. There is still time left in this inward season, and time for signs of new life inside to communicate and assert itself.

Semaphore

Now a memory returns:
In the rearview mirror I see him waving us off,
A continuous gesture
In the manner of some pint-size apostle,
Arms and hands crossing back and forth in front,
A familial signal
 For comings and goings.
I remember waving back, choking on tears
For the power of the moment,
And that image has stayed with me,
Even as we have faded from each other's view.
It now feels eternal,
Telling, haunting, reminding,
That from our first conscious moment
We are, each of us,
Small children waving goodbye.

February 13...

I TAKE THE SAME WALK IN THE WOODS, pretty much every day no matter what the weather. It is a grounding routine and a retreat into nature, which seems to provide a special comfort. There have been days when I walk and sob, days when I feel a sort of meditative neutrality, and days when awe or even joy creep back in. The conditions are as variable as New England weather: icy and gray today, sunny and bright the next. The last time I was out we had just had a big snowfall and the sun had just returned with its blue sky. A soft wind blew snow like glitter through the woods. The limbs of the large maples wore a beautiful fresh coat of snow and made supplicating gestures up towards the sun, which answered with its shafts of light. There was a beauty there that could cut through layers of grief and somehow intermingle with that grief in a way that did not feel paradoxical.

It is not just the beautiful moments that provide the comfort. I think it is more simply the act of walking and following a trail. No matter what is happening externally or internally, you put one foot in front of the other, slow or fast, with ease or effort. And isn't that life—the act of proceeding no matter what? Perhaps this is what I am ritualizing and signifying out there on some level, with that spectrum of life all around—growth, decay, harshness and beauty.

We had our eighteen-week ultrasound last week, which couldn't have better encapsulated the experience of simultaneous grieving and growing. Before the procedure even began we were emotionally undone by the mere fact of being back in the same hospital where we brought Ryland for all his appointments. The sound of the Velcro on the blood pressure cuff vividly brought back memories of all the times we checked on his vital signs, up through the last time at death. I don't know where the water comes from anymore, but there is always a deluge of tears at the ready. We proceed with looking at this new life, and every feeling and tear intermingle: the awe of seeing a wiggly, human form, the excruciating flashbacks of MRIs, the suspense of checking on things, the profound relief that for this little life all looked well. And then we learn we are having another little boy. Cue another deluge, where all streams merge into one.

Whom do I thank for this gift? That little X and Y pair? An all-powerful force with a poetic sensibility? Did you have something to do with this, Ryland? And who is this brave little soul coming to join with these wounded ones? All I know is that I have carried brothers with more to teach than I could have ever foreseen or imagined.

Apprehension

Leaving the hospital early on in the game,
My granddaughter asked,
"Poppi, where do people go when they die",
A not so veiled expression of concern for her little brother
And the essential question of humankind
Coming, at that moment, from a four year old.
It occurs to me that we may compose that question
As very young children
And then spend the length of our subsequent years
Ignoring it,
Filled to the waking brim
With quotidian concerns and pursuits,
Constructing expectations and achieving goals
Until an entire lifetime goes by and we wonder,
What was it all for?
Maybe my granddaughter's question needs
A more prominent place in the mind,
A motto inscribed to remind that
The facts of life are bound
By the facts of death.
Maybe death needs to become
A more constant companion,
Teaching, clarifying, providing perspective,
So that we never, ever miss apprehending
The miracle of each sentient moment.

February 26...

I HAVE BEEN COMPILING BABY PHOTOS OF RYLAND to make an album. For so long it was too hard to look at images of the past, before cancer so violently changed our trajectory. For some reason I am able to look at the infant images now; perhaps there is a distance there that helps. It is indeed like looking at a former life. The infancy themes captured in those photos are comforting: the awe and love in everyone's eyes, the intimacy and tenderness of all that affection and holding, the delicious body of a baby, and the incredible self and soul that emerge with the passing weeks.

He looked so strong, even as a baby. His robust form most likely carried him through his perilous delivery relatively unscathed. I know that the pictures will, for a while, document a healthy growing boy who meets his milestones and then some. But then there will be a turning point: a picture of him with a hospital band, and then the evidence of steroids and compromise. Though we lived through all of that in the most direct, hands-on way, it is nevertheless agonizing to see his illness creep into our visual history, to see our lives divided into a before and after. It reminds me of the feelings I had when he was first diagnosed—that there had been this most sinister plot in the making and that we were these sitting ducks completely unaware and unprepared for our fate. Rationally I can accept that his tumor was not some sort of evil creation, but rather biology run amok; however, the feeling lingers, in memory and image, of a terrible wrong committed on an otherwise flourishing young child and family.

The final pictures of Ryland in some ways mirror the infancy ones: lots of sleeping in the arms of loved ones. But the round lines and rolls are gone, in exchange for a withering frame and gaunt face. For all the time I spent tending and caressing and loving that form, I now feel gutted when I look at the picture: How can this happen to my baby? You are hardwired to nurture and protect, and that is what the early pictures show: all the nursing and feeding and bathing and cuddling. But then impossibly, we had to watch him lose everything, including the swallow reflex which, with the deprivation of food and water, would usher in his final week. And we did watch—we stared down everything at the time because that is what you do, you go anywhere with and for your child. But now that it is over, the trauma of that experience asserts itself and remains, and I wonder what you end up doing with it. How do you integrate an experience that we are not made to bear as human beings? Does time truly soften the edges, and would it even feel right or true to have those edges feel soft in any way?

If I had to describe life right now, I would say it feels like walking along the edge of a canyon: My footing feels somewhat secure, but there is always that risk of the land crumbling and giving way. I avoid the fall when I avoid those difficult images and memories. However, avoidance and distance are clearly not the routes to real healing. I suppose my life challenge will entail becoming a more able and fit hiker, who can make those descents and come back up and be able to acclimate to the elevation and terrain changes so as to keep going, forever integrating all parts of the trail into this mysterious life journey.

Side Effects

This cocktail of grief and pain
Has caused me the opposing side effects
Of a sharpened attention
And a leaden stupor,
Not dissolved together in a moment
But alternating
In certain indeterminate stretches of time
And happening
Involuntarily, or so it seems.
If one of these symptoms should persist,
Become part of my permanent condition
(Although I don't yet know how it will happen),
Perhaps I will find with it
Some comfort and sustenance.
After all, what better salve for pain
Than apprehending,
In one glorious instant,
The simultaneous pivot
Of a thousand birds in flight?

March 26...

LAST WEEK WE HAD ANOTHER BIG SNOWSTORM, giving the first day of spring the appearance of mid-January. With my emotional attachment to winter, which has felt almost synonymous with my state of grief, I felt almost relieved by this fresh layer of white blanketing any signs of life that might feel too discordant with Ryland's ever-present loss. Hiking through the woods that day, I took on the effort of breaking trail, again, through the deep snow while taking in the beauty of the first sun after a winter storm. What quickly became palpable was the heat of this sun, which seemed to be sending a reassurance that spring was in fact coming despite all appearances. The bird calls reiterated this promise. And I thought to myself, this is how nature holds death and life at the same time, in this lovely, seamless way. And I observed my own body—my gaping, wounded heart just above this expanding, round belly. Physically, I felt like a mirror of the earth around me and there was some comfort in that.

These are the moments of peace that feel like steppingstones across sorrow's wide river. They do not appear often enough to keep me out of the water but they do allow for a moment of rest, and hope. Hope for what, it is hard to say. Not for "moving on" or "letting go," as that can never happen with this love. Perhaps it is the hope for a full integration of Ryland's life in my own, in such a way that the intensity of my love is not always felt with an equally intense pain.

This makes me think of the pain of looking at photographs. It is like looking at the sun, which draws you to it with its warmth and beauty, but that burns and hurts a direct gaze. The photos we hang are supposed to be mirrors of our family life, not reminders of that life that was taken. I want to look at my child—how many hours did I spend staring at him when he was alive, completely undone by his perfection? I do not want to turn away from his image now, unable to endure the pain. But the image is not Ryland. Right now I want to think of him not as a static snapshot, forever held in the frame of the past, but rather as an entity that continues to exist, as someone with whom I will always have a growing relationship. So, while I will look at pictures, when I truly want to be with him I must go inward. I must shut my eyes so as not to burn and feel his warm spirit and bask in his beauty that I know is there. This is how I will welcome spring.

Photograph

Six months out I remain at a loss and out of answers.
The grief books accurately predicted
Lengthening intervals of peace,
Yet the moments of intense missing
Are as debilitating as ever,
And now all those tender images tease and taunt
For what was and what might have been.
The photo in my bathroom haunts daily,
He in my arms facing the camera
And my head burrowed into his.
At that point a month before his death
He has a rare look of sadness and resignation,
While I, much less brave, can face
Neither the camera nor the inevitable.
There we are, bound up in a life and death drama,
A tableau ancient and inexorable.
It will likely torment forever
That I can't somehow re-stage that tableau,
Re-write the narrative
So that our roles could have, rightfully, been reversed.

April 9...

Maybe this isn't so new, but I have just been feeling so weepy. I feel like the loss and the sorrow are settling into my bones, are weaving themselves into my DNA, and that the body is responding with this flow of tears from the deepest of pools. Unbelievably, almost six months have passed since I held Ryland though I don't really know how to process the markers of time. It could have been yesterday that he was here, or was it another life? Only in occasional dreams can I go back to the utmost pleasure and relief of "seeing" him in the here and now. I know that grief, and my relationship with Ryland, cannot be described in any temporal sense, but rather in the way they evolve and express themselves in my own soul and body. There is so much shifting within: my identity, my relationship to life, not to mention my very organs as my belly grows and grows.

How ironic that I had always declared limbo my nemesis, that my comfort zone, from childhood, had tended to demand organization. Now there appears to be no choice but to surrender to chaos and upheaval and unpredictability. Perhaps the difference now is that these things do not impose the same fear—they are intrinsic to my ability to live with what has happened and to continue to connect with Ryland.

On a recent warm day, I was thinking more about what spring means to me this year. I was thinking how good it felt not to brace against the cold, and what a relief it was to relax my shoulders and jaw and joints into the heat of the sun. It all made me think about this surrender to life, even if that means that grief's waters run hard and free through the psyche like a river charging with mountain runoff. This may not be a season of exultation as much as an often painful but necessary and exquisite opening up to a life I did not plan, whatever that might look like.

I have frequently asked myself, "How does one live with pain like this?" It's probably the first question of most parents who have lost a child, or of those who ponder that possibility. But of course, pain is part of living, even this kind of pain, at any unforeseen juncture. Life darkens, but also deepens as it throws back curtains of expectations and assumptions and asks: How do you accept the unacceptable, bear the unbearable, and live through whatever is in store?

May 5, Mother's Day Address...

North Chapel, Woodstock, Vermont

THE LAST TIME I STOOD IN THIS SPOT WAS NOVEMBER OF LAST YEAR, to say goodbye to my son Ryland, taken by cancer at age three. As I did, I knew there was a new life beginning to form within, a sibling who had shared this planet with his brother for a couple of weeks. Such an unbelievable irony that rapidly dividing cells can wreak such havoc and hold such promise.

Thank goodness for winter, for a dark, quiet gestational period for both my grief and for the task of making room, emotionally and physically, for new life. How to fully grieve and fully grow simultaneously—this was not a topic in which I was well versed, not a chapter in a typical pregnancy book I might have read the first time around. I would need every day of the long Vermont winter to begin to plod slowly through this riddle, and never have I been so grateful for the length of that season as well as for the length of a pregnancy.

At Ryland's service, Daniel had beautifully captured that royal pickle we parents find ourselves in—so much vulnerability and danger in attaching too strongly to things in this life. But how do we not do that with our little babies, with our children? Nature has that thoroughly rigged, with those little toes and that smell of a baby's head, with every hormone and instinct that is activated. And even as that baby grows and becomes more independent, that attachment remains, to this curious and enchanting little spirit that has come into your life and then comes into his own. I vividly remember staring at my daughter Jane soon after she was born, sleeping peacefully in her little bassinette. I guess the active imagination of a new parent had started to kick in as I started to think of all the things in life from which I could not protect her, and was reduced to tears. My father found me in this state, and with a loving and knowing and slightly apologetic look he informed me that yes indeed I was now officially a "hostage to fortune."

In some ways, there was no rational reason to plunge into a pregnancy amidst so much despair. How could we possibly make ourselves even more vulnerable? How could we possibly have any shred of trust left in life when our son had been so cruelly afflicted? I suppose the decision did not come from a highly rational place but rather from the same place that declares that yes, I would endure every ounce of pain and heartache of the last nineteen months for the deep privilege and greatest joy of knowing my little Ryland.

So no need to wrap my head around this mystifying state of death and birth—as long as I can wrap my soul around it, and that the body, in its ancient wisdom, can hold the opposites in one place. There are moms I have met here at church who have walked similar roads—losing a child, and perhaps not having children after that but, somehow, slowly, opening back up to life, a new life at that—despite wounds that feel utterly unbearable. I am grateful for their empathy and for their examples of strength. My own mother too, suffering the double blow of her grandson's incurable disease and her daughter's incurable anguish, somehow marches forward with that impossible weight, still puts her heart out, still accesses the possibility of joy for the future even when I have been at my most guarded.

And let me also acknowledge the great mother too, the earth who is thankfully such an available consultant and guide in this part of the country. Walking the same woods daily throughout the year, I am reminded of the cycles that flow in a seamless way, of how life and death relate to each other and are in fact contained in one place, in one system. May might be a fitting time, in some ways, for Mother's Day, with all its life bursting forth. But in the woods back in March (that month that is not a typical favorite) I remember observing mother earth at perhaps her most magical: warm shafts of sun and bird calls emerging after a snow storm, tiny green sprouts pushing through a thick brown blanket of dead leaves.

And so all mothers are charged with supporting life's spectrum, with holding on and letting go, with loving and attaching at the risk of great pain. We carry a baby until it is time for birth, we support him until he can sit, hold hands until he can walk, and on and on. For some, we hold and comfort until a last breath is drawn. But even under the ashes of what must have been our destruction, there is the drumbeat of an eternal love, fierce and tender, forever encompassing all it has known.

May 24...

Dear Ryland,

PERHAPS YOU HAVE NOTICED MY NESTING BEHAVIORS and my strategy of gearing up to do your room by first organizing every other room in the house. Maybe this helped to a point but there were some false assumptions. First, that there are any real emotionally benign spaces. Even that dirty old mudroom contains your beautiful self—your John Deere hat hanging on a hook, your school backpack still supplied with an extra diaper and change of clothes. And then of course there was really no way to desensitize myself to the power of your room, your personal space, your things. Not that I really wanted to fully desensitize. I guess I am content to flow between sadness and a certain numbness, and, sometimes, find some state of grace in between those places where I feel everything and somehow feel okay. But it is a lot for the human heart, especially at a time of preparation for birth when you want to feel safe, prepared, in control.

But you are where you are. And the nesting for your brother, like the pregnancy, will contain sadness. Who will this child be, born of so much intense emotion? I am becoming curious. All I know is he is big and robust. He likes to move a lot after dinner; and he wakes up in the morning shortly after the rest of us, while we are all together in bed. It's rather cute.

Please, Ryland, if you see me scrubbing your furniture and your toys, know that I am not scrubbing you out of them, I am not trying to wash you away. When I found some of your old shirts, still with remains of food drool, I could barely bring myself to wash them. I want you here, I want you part of our family's life, however that is possible. I want to feel your presence in a way that transcends "things." But things retain their power, don't they? The flannel pants you wore at the end of life for warmth, your favorite vehicles and books. Perhaps the most loaded thing for me is the red, pedal-less "lil' rocket" bike we got for you when you turned two. You were so agile on that so quickly, even if your feet hardly reached the ground. Then you became sick, and the bike was put away until last summer when we helped you balance on it. Do you remember one night in bed when we were cuddling, you asked me softly: "Mom, will I ever be able to ride my bike by myself?" And I said, "I don't know, but we will always be here to help you." Oh sweetie-pie, I cannot stop crying.

It is remarkable to me that your life was so short, numerically speaking. Going through your clothes, I am struck by how small they look—the two-to-three-year-old stuff. In some ways I feel like you were so much older, that we have known each other for lifetimes. Could that be true? Can you confirm that from where you are? I feel like I have lost a soul mate…and then I hope that, in fact, I haven't really lost you at all.

Palimpsest

This odd, wonderful word comes to me
In the middle of the night,
An elliptical gift from a school colleague long ago,
And the intrigue of its sound on the lips
Is as compelling as its etymology:
From the Greek 'palimpsestos, rubbed again',
Meaning a text that bears the traces of erased texts
That came before.
So today when my wife embraced
A dear friend's young grandson,
Her earnest tears made clear
The palimpsest of that singular moment,
When the antecedent,
In the form of her own lost grandson
Was revealed so vividly
In the living boy,
The trace, the trace
Of the erasure still so evident on the slate.

This will be the case for some long time,
When our encounters with shining little children,
Who remind us of the prior text,
Will require the opening of arms
To gratefully receive messages writ clear.

June 6...

Dear Ryland,

A YEAR AGO YOU BROKE YOUR LEG and would never walk again. That was the beginning of everything being taken from you. You always did what you could with everything you had: pedaling on your bike with your feet taped to the pedals, moving around like a frog with your fisted hands and pulling your two legs together behind you, pointing to the upstairs to request a bath when you couldn't speak and when the bath offered that bit of comfort, and living off Jell-O for a while when it was the only thing you could swallow. I tried to be right there with you, wherever you were at, to relish in what you could do. It all almost feels harder looking back now at all the many losses you endured. The trauma of that as a parent seems to sink in more when you are no longer in the moment of coping and dealing and adapting. Now it just literally breaks my heart to think about it, and the memories revive the questions: Why? Was this your fate? Or was this the gravest injustice? Will an answer ever come? Your birth was such a triumph of life over death; it is still unbelievable that death returned with such strength and certainty.

In a couple weeks I will be giving birth again. Life has been so beguiling I find my mind clear of expectations. Will everything be all right? I don't know. I am looking forward to meeting your little brother; I think he must be special to come along when he did. I trust that my heart will grow such that my love and devotion to you will never feel compromised by that which I feel for this new life. I want you to know that as I hold and caress this new being, you will be there too. I will always be doing the same for you, my first little boy.

Tractor

I was attempting to fashion a tractor-boat,
A small wooden something to commemorate my departed grandson,
A token we will float down a river
With joy and sorrow on his birthday.

But first I needed a template for my vessel,
An image of his favorite vehicle to copy,
When on some cosmic cue,
Here comes the local farmer to hay our field,
Riding a John Deere that fits the bill.
It's perfect: the black and green and yellow color scheme
And the proportions
That I can easily make nautical.

What I soon realize and remember, though, is
That the farmer has recently lost his own wife
To something close to my grandson's disease,
Another life claimed too soon by dreadful circumstance.
And so I know
He rides the tractor with tears and pain and memories
That conform to mine.

In his earnest effort to hay the field,
He gives me my template for the tractor-boat
And a reminder
That we all ply common ground,
Mysterious and beyond our understanding.

The farmer appears a stoic on his machine,
Dispatching bales with a beautiful efficiency,
While my own crude facsimile emerges:
Chassis, wheels, cockpit,
And a mast ready for sailing.

June 25...

HAPPY BIRTHDAY, DARLING RYLAND. You would be turning four today, though I needn't be stuck on the number: You know I know you are an old soul, a timeless spirit, with an impact that far, far exceeds your impossibly short time with us.

We ate lemon cake for breakfast and sang to you. Jane picked out a number four candle at the store. We treasured pictures and memories of you. We laughed and cried. We went to the White Cottage with Nonni, Poppi, Richard and a few others…and we ordered hot dogs and floated a "tractor boat" down the river. We went to your gravesite and lit some sparklers…other friends had left some pretty shells with loving messages written on them for you. We went down to Rainbow School and saw all the teachers in their Run4Ryland t-shirts, and we sat on your special bench in your garden outside that they have planted and named for you. We went to Bo's house for dinner and toasted to you.

Daddy and I awoke early this morning, ahead of your birth time of 5:30 am. I could feel your little brother wake up five minutes before. Memories of your dramatic birth remain so vivid—the miracle baby, who will always be my little miracle.

The weather today—foggy, then sunny and hot, then stormy and rainy and foggy again—seemed to mirror all the emotions swirling around in all of us. So much to feel all at once. In three days your brother is due to be born.

You will be there too.

July 6...

Dear Ryland,

Your little brother Silas was born on June 28, about one week ago. He is very cute—you would love him and be such a wonderful big brother I know. As all-consuming as a newborn can be, you have been constantly on my mind too, of course. Being back on the floor where you were born brought up so much for Dad and me, and I also found myself drawing strength from you as we proceeded with the planned C-section. We have all called Silas "Ryland" a few times, and I sometimes feel transported back to newborn days with you. Sometimes I feel like I am living out a second life, without being able to finish the first.

While Silas definitely has his own look, there are certainly flashbacks involved with having a little baby boy again, roughly your size with the dark newborn hair and emerging blue eyes. Your birthdays are three days apart, so the seasonal experience is the same, right down to the wet summer conditions that we also had back in 2009. It can almost make the last three-plus years feel like a dream, but not really; the intensity of your loss is so easily summoned, my love for you as distinct and fierce as ever. The acute grief of the beginning months may feel somewhat tempered by time, but new developments also have a way of ushering in a new set of losses, as in thinking about what an amazing big brother you would be and, with the addition of a newborn, what a great pal for Jane.

Silas will always have a big brother, and I guess we will just have to see how that plays out in his life. For now, when he smiles and chuckles and grimaces in his sleep, I like to imagine the two of you communing and you perhaps offering him a little primer on life. I often find myself nursing Silas on the same couch cushion where I held you as you passed away, and I like to think of that spot as a sort of portal connecting you both. When I soothe and care for him now, I imagine and hope that you are somehow receiving that too…all that nurturing and protecting that I still want to give to you.

In connecting her grief over one profound, familial loss to a larger circle of environmental plights and concerns, the writer Terry Tempest Williams observes that, "Grief dares us to love once more." Amidst all the myriad emotions that will forever color this life, I think that this sentiment needs to be fundamental, for you Ryland, for Silas, for everyone.

Medicine Man

I gave you this glib moniker, Silas,
Soon after you were born,
Thinking wishfully that you might have
The curative power to help heal
The wounded souls who are your family.
Was this too much to ask?
Only weeks old
You have all the nascent charms that beguile and distract
In the most soothing way,
So, my little healer, you're off
To a good start.
Yet in time you will come to know
What is rarely said within your family but deeply understood:
That your brother helped give you your life,
Conspired in your conception,
And thereby (in ironic symbiosis) ensured
This current vocation that may necessarily
Last your lifetime.
Whether gift or debt or burden
There's no telling yet
How you may receive this knowledge,
But you do come from a stouthearted lot.
My guess, my wish, my hope is that you carry
Your kin's mantle with the ease
Of spring's first vital breath on your shoulder.

August 30...

Dear Ryland,

WE ARE JUST BACK FROM A FEW WEEKS IN RHODE ISLAND. How we missed you on the beach. The first summer there without you brought up all the expected longings and questions—what would Ryland be up to these days? Would he love the water like his sister or be more of a sand play guy? Those wonderings often feel so painful and sad, and tend to bring up the injustice of your disease over and over again.

At one point, though, I did feel this deep peacefulness that accompanied the feeling that you were with me and everywhere. I was walking down Round Pond Road the first day and just felt this strong presence. The feelings of peace and pain are not static; they ebb and flow like the waves.

With Silas in the picture and this new family constellation, it can feel like we are starting a new life, with the concurrent feeling that my old one remains unfinished. Silas's little spirit is unfolding before us: We are on the adventure of discovering who he is, but already I know he is just the one who needs to be here. Poppi has called him "Medicine Man" and I think that works. He is really cute, with traces of us all I would say, but he is his own little guy. He exudes both fun and calm, with deep twinkly eyes like yours. The only thing missing is his big brother.

I had a dream recently that you, your dad and I were in an apartment together (one I did not recognize) and we had you go into a narrow room with a big window looking out on some city. You climbed onto a blue couch, and then we shut the door to keep a dog out (it may have been my dog Sophie from childhood). Then we left the apartment and went to some other home in another neighborhood. Suddenly I was gripped with panic that you were there alone—wondering what you were doing, and why didn't we allow the dog in at least for company. The dream ended with me not being able to bear not being with you, and I was going to go back, though this didn't occur in the dream. I awoke with the despair, as a mother, of not being able to go to you.

I hope you do not feel abandoned, dear Ryland. Have I shut you off too much in my mind in order to care for this little baby? I don't know. I feel like you are on my mind always, though maybe now in a different way than the depths of grief that ensued just after your passing. I don't cry all the time now, but I never feel far from the abyss.

October 15...

Dear Ryland,

TODAY IS MY FIRST BIRTHDAY WITHOUT YOU, and we are a week away from the anniversary of your departure from us. What a month, October. It obviously feels so different to me now; it has so many dimensions. There are still the birthdays, the bounty of the harvest, the colors—all the things that always gave it magic. But the fleeting nature of it all is so much more intense for me now—a blaze of color, but then it's gone, apples on the tree until they fall, growth in the garden until it is all over for a long time. I don't mean for this to sound depressing—it is more like a realization that life was always like this and now I just understand. You are our guide to living in the moment and living fully while we can.

A couple more bits of magic about this time: wooly bears and milkweed fairies. I choose to focus on them and retain a childlike attitude alongside the other heavier emotions.

I remember a year ago you ate your last "meal," which at the time meant I would drop Jell-O into your mouth as you lay on my lap. You did not eat after my birthday. Thank you for that final gift to me. It could not have been easy to eat that way, with your swallow reflex pretty much gone, but I was at least able to nurture you in that most basic maternal way. I think of that as I feed your little brother.

I have so much sadness locked up. I let it out when it needs to but there is a lifetime of sadness that will always be there. Sometimes it hides behind a lingering shock—did that really happen—but shock is just a shield for pain. That pain can rush in any time, like the other day on the way to the grocery store. But then did you see the acts of kindness there? The older woman who was so drawn to your little brother and looked directly at me and said he was gift. And then the kind woman behind me in line who helped me with my things as I worried about being so cumbersome with my stroller etc. I don't use heaven and angel speak that often but all I could think of was that there were angels in the grocery store that day. Sometimes it seems like just when life feels way too hard, there is some little gift of hope or infusion of relief.

I miss you today and every day. I think of you constantly. In this way, I do feel we have a close, ongoing relationship. But of course I have to wonder—what would your little four-year-old self be doing and looking like now? I would love to know.

October 22...

WHAT IS A YEAR? Today it seems equally equivalent to an hour as to a lifetime. Memories of you can feel so vivid that you feel eternally present though at the same time every moment without you here represents an unacceptable distance, and it can feel like forever since I held you close. Grief, like love, does not want to be understood or measured in a temporal sense. But here we are at the one-year anniversary of your departure, and that timing begs to be felt and recognized.

A year ago, almost to the minute, I held you here in this same room in which I now write, as you took those dramatic final breaths. I remember trying to reassure you that is was okay to go but then my echoing wail gave away my true feelings when I thought you had taken your last breath, which happened to be your second to last. I worried that you heard my cry in your final moment, and that it made for a more anxious and fearful transition than I ever would have wanted for you. But now I hope that you realize that that cry was the only form my breath could take right then, and that it came from the deepest depth of love.

What else do I hope for a year later? That the image of you in your final days—your wasted, precious body—no longer reflects where you are. This image may always have the power to tear a mother in two, and may always hang on with the vice grip of trauma. But I want to believe that you have sailed far beyond the ravages of disease and death, and that you truly are at peace and safe in hands more capable than my own.

And for the living, for myself? I don't know if peace and safety feel like plausible goals in this world. Your loss will always be a wound. How can the loss of a child be anything but? The hemorrhage of a year ago may have stopped and some scar tissue may have formed, but the wound will always have the most tender of centers. And the challenge now seems to be—how to move through life with this wound, how to bear the pain, when to nurse it, when to push through it. Ultimately, it becomes a question of meaning: How will this injury that cannot fully heal guide me in a way that honors you and gives purpose to our days? At this one year anniversary, and perhaps for many more anniversaries to come, we will sit with more questions than answers and aspire to a child's mind and heart akin to yours—open and curious, instinctual and non-judgmental. We had three short years together, but from what I can tell, your legacy has no bounds.

November 25...

Dear Ryland,

WHAT A GIFT IT IS TO DREAM of you at night—like a miraculous visit. It doesn't happen as often as I would like, but it is so powerful when you do appear. So different than my daily conscious thoughts of you, which are pretty constant and flow from my own familiar waking mind. The dreams feel more like a meeting in another place with messages to receive and deduce. They make me feel most connected to an afterlife or a separate place where we can still be together.

Last night in my dream I heard you calling "Mama" from a bed, ready to be picked up. I picked you up and held you—it was essentially that simple. But the connection I felt to you, the twinkle in your eye, your radiant smile—they filled the dream with so much depth and joy. I recall knowing that you had your illness in the dream, but that you were defying its progress. You were still able to talk a bit (oh, to hear you say my name), you seemed pretty strong physically, and fully alert and healthy looking. There was a feeling that perhaps the illness would stop there and that I would have you in that state forever. So glorious. But then to wake and re-enter reality and miss you so intensely. I will go to our dream places in my mind. Please keep visiting me.

Hard to fathom that we will have our second Thanksgiving without you this week. The first holidays are all over, and while there may be some relief in having those very painful firsts behind us, there is now the feeling of greater distance, which makes me ache. Your marker stone finally went in the ground at your gravesite a few weeks ago. There is probably a reason it took us a year to do it. The permanency of that stone with your name and dates is so hard to take in. We have kept the more "alive" seeming elements there, the sand castle, and shells and rocks, and plants.

Did you see Jane as she encountered your stone for the first time? I was in the car with Silas, and she trotted over there in her ballet tights and tutu, and mud boots and fleece. And I watched as she looked very thoughtfully, and then lay on the stone as if to embrace you. Then she blew some bubbles all around. She loves you so deeply as we all do. She has also opened her heart to brother Silas, too. I would think it would take some bravery to love and bond again. But she is a brave girl and he is a very loveable fellow. He will know you and love you too.

December 22...

I MISS YOU MISS YOU MISS YOU. You remain on my mind all the time, though these unexpected and strong reminders happen sometimes and throw me...like when Jane made a sound of exasperation tonight and sounded just like you or when the quality of little Silas's voice sounded like yours through the phone. These moments bring both comfort in the sense that you will always share our blood and be connected to us. But they also bring pain in how they accentuate your absence and make me long for the one and only you.

Does time heal or does it just transform pain in a way that can make it feel like healing is happening? Maybe I don't cry daily, maybe I can do things for pleasure now and not have it feel totally wrong or odd. But beneath all the scar tissue, layers and layers of it, it still seems that there is a wound that will always be very raw. Your pictures continue to kill me as do the memories of your struggle. The acute trauma may be behind us, the utter shock of your leaving, but the aftershocks can break up whatever firm ground we lay down, and the utter truth of your death just seems to burrow deeper and deeper into my being which still does not want to play host to such a horror.

I wish death were not such a mystery, that I could know with confidence that you were somewhere safe, and somewhere I could see you again. I wish there were more signs. The ones I hold on to are from that night a little over a year ago. It was that night I was in so much distress...I just remember crying in the shower, pleading with you to tell me you were okay. Later we heard those strange "footsteps" upstairs (not Jane's, as she was asleep). And then those two marvelous dreams that I still remember so clearly. The first had us in a big, ornate, European style station or terminal bustling with people. I think we were gathered with folks from your pre-school but then the two of us got on a bike together and rode off on to a big bridge. We pedaled up with people all around. As we crested the top you became worried about the impending descent, and I reassured you by making it fun and turning it into a game: "Hold my thumbs and pretend they are ski poles and you will ski down!" This seemed to work and the dream ended with us at the top of the bridge with only blue sky ahead.

In the second dream (these seemed to be back-to-back) I was walking around in what was apparently your old Rainbow School though it looked different. I went from the indoor classrooms to outside where I passed a big pigpen where kids were playing in the mud, and then approached a beautiful, pristine pool which looked very inviting in the sunny weather. I saw you on the other end of the pool—the deep end—and dove in and swam to you. You jumped in to me, and at first I was worried I could not hold you because you had all your clothes on. But I was able to hold you and swim with you easily, and the dream ended with us smiling together in the water.

These dreams felt like gifts and visitations and communications, and I don't use those terms casually. They are still enduring images and places of true comfort. I wish my days and nights were full of such powerful signs of something being okay.

But for now I will treasure these.

January 6...

If you ask me now, I can honestly say, I don't know how I did it. I look, quickly as if any longer would cause unbearable harm, at the picture of us: I am pushing you on a large truck in a sandbox. We are both smiling but the cancer is there too, in your lean, in your curled toes. The smiles were, I suppose, for that moment of boyhood fun, but the picture breaks my heart into smaller and smaller pieces as I think what was taken from you, as I think of that broken promise of a life alongside the other kids in the sandbox. It can be hard, at times, to shake the cruel feeling that I betrayed you, bringing you into the world and building all that sense of promise and trust, just to have your body turn on you in such gruesome ways. Of course I wanted nothing but a long and happy journey for you, and I did have such shining visions of your future. You had a breathtaking beauty and soul, perhaps not of this world after all.

But to be given this awe-inspiring gift, to have it broken and taken—what to make of this? Do we even try to take lessons—lessons in non-clinging, in love in the here and now—or do we feel the full weight of the trauma and the pain? Both, I suppose. But there are these jarring moments when the trauma prevails, when the full force of the pain rushes back in almost with more intensity without the shock to protect us. How did I do it? How did I ever watch you die? How did I ever release your body from my arms for a final time and let you leave this house? It will never make sense.

January 19...

AGAIN, SO LOVELY TO SEE YOU IN MY DREAMS, dear Ryland. It may have been prompted in part by your brother, who wakes quite often in the night to nurse (just like his siblings). In my dream, I was aware of someone's cries in the night, and when I left the room, I discovered you in your crib, right there in the hallway, where everything was cast in a light blue light. You were dressed in a familiar light blue onesie. Standing in your crib, with your short curly blonde hair, you appeared perhaps just barely two years old (pre-diagnosis, then). You were holding the rails and with excited energy you were sort of running in place. I said something playful to the effect of, "Are you going for a jog, Ryland?!" I then had a quick flash of questioning about how I should handle this situation best as a parent, in terms of getting you back to sleep. But then this wave of relief and joy came with the conclusion of: "Who cares?! I get to hold Ryland and I am going to walk him up and down this hallway!"

I awoke before doing so, but I emerged from sleep with at least the intention and possibility...the promise?...of holding you again. My waking hours now contain both the lingering joy of that next step, as well as the throbbing ache of not being able to do it physically, now.

However these dreams leave me, I love to see you and to feel like we have this beautiful, unfolding relationship, albeit in another place. I prefer the freshness, the aliveness of the dreams to the images of the past, to that life of ours cut so short. I prefer the feeling in dreams of no distance, no space, no time gone by.

I must say, though time does march along, you continue to have a constant presence for me throughout my days. I wonder how much other people may realize that—just how constantly I think of you, even when doing or talking about other things. And like in the dream, this creates a simultaneous comfort and ache, a sort of infinite spiraling of loving and longing, of connecting and missing, that I know will be with me for all of my days.

Ryland's Wheel

I'm willing to subscribe to the notion
That he was exceptional,
That, as many have suggested, he accomplished much
In three short years,
An old soul cycling in and out of our lives long enough
To remind about care and joy and bravery.

Even before he was sick, Ryland was
The "Newmalama", with movie star looks
And a guru's gentle spirit.
To be sure he had little boy fascinations,
Especially with ordinary wheeled vehicles,
Tractors and the like,
But now his life will forever conjure up thoughts
Of entirely bigger wheels:
A great circle of people moved by his story,
Then an even greater arc that connects all of us in this life,
And beyond that perhaps something infinitely circular and reincarnate,
Whereby we rotate endlessly back into this world
From some other pure, numinous realm.
The last idea is a stretch for me,
But Ryland's made a good case for it.

The advent of a younger sibling presently moves
Our family circle one more degree,
And I dare to believe
That from some righteous vantage point on a magnificent arc
Ryland summons us
To accept, with courage and love, the gift
That is now his brother's turn to give.

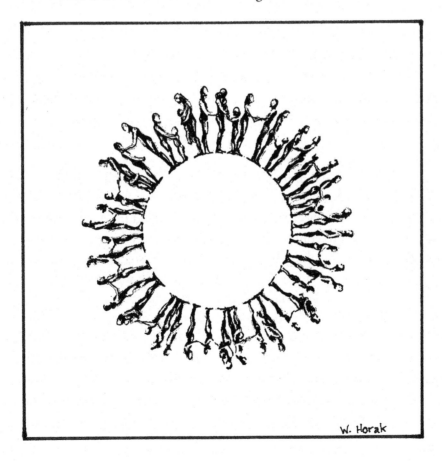

W. Horak

February 3...

Jane will turn seven in a couple weeks. This will be her second birthday without her first little brother. In many ways, she is showing the exuberance of any young child at birthday time, making party plans and gleefully anticipating presents. But then a comment will reveal her loss and longing right beneath the surface, as when she requested a lemon cake with a special chocolate decoration like you had, Ryland, on your third birthday. She explained that her "greatest wish" is to have you here, but because that is not possible she wants to have this particular cake in your honor.

This moment gave me the vision of grief as Russian stacking dolls. On the surface we have resumed a sort of normal living which somehow, unbelievably, includes joys and fun again. And what a relief to see this happen for Jane, to see her thrive at school and become an enthusiastic skier and forge loving relationships. But of course there will always be layers of grief below. At those outer layers, perhaps we can smile at certain stories of you, imbuing memory with a kind of sweetness. But as you go just a little deeper, the memories begin to hurt. For me, I think of that moment, so clear to me still, during your initial hospitalization when you awoke in your crib in your purple hospital gown with monitors all around you. You simply said "Mommy? Daddy?" with a voice of pure sweetness and innocence. You were ready to be picked up and snuggled as you started your day. You did not know that our lives had just been so horribly and irrevocably changed. We alone harbored this knowledge, the knowledge that we could not stomach but had to contain as we snuggled and loved you.

Jane recently revealed a vulnerable place of her own when she described how the school gymnasium can make her sad because that is where she was when she was pulled from school the day you died. That memory seems to be clear as day for her. And then of course there were the unfolding events after that when she came home to find you passed away in my arms and we all cried together. It stuns me now to think that she, at five years old, spent an afternoon paying final respects and saying last goodbyes to your deceased body. I suppose I must accept that this did indeed happen, but I may never deem it acceptable. And that is what that innermost layer of grief feels like—a nugget of exquisite pain that cannot be fully described, maybe not even fully borne. So you create protective layers around it, this tender egg at the core of your being surrounded by a nest of all matters of coping.

I will say that Jane seems to be a sturdy little Russian doll, and perhaps just the kind of soul to endure this unexpected road. She has an open heart and mind, and a compassionate nature that gives me hope that her grief can find some meaningful and beautiful expression.

Silas, too, may be just the one who needs to be here. At seven months, he is showing us more and more of who he is—sweet, funny, affectionate, easy-going, and highly capable of making everyone smile. I know some may see you in him but truth be told, I think he is distinctly himself. Certainly these attributes could describe you too, but they manifested in ways that were purely your own. It feels to me that Silas is not trying to be you at all, maybe out of deference to you and your irreplaceability. No, he is a whole new soul entirely, and we are beginning to see who he is, and to discover how this bright little star fits into our family constellation.

March 6...

I WAS INTERVIEWED BY A WOMAN at the hospital recently, in anticipation of Poppi's donation of his sculpture, *Ryland's Wheel*, to the pediatric oncology floor. Going back over the history of your illness, I felt a wave of fresh grief, strong and penetrating.

Perhaps it had to do with speaking with someone new to the story or perhaps it flowed from the thoughtful and compassionate space the interviewer provided me to explain and feel. Who knows? But while painful and hard, the feelings also felt so true, like a more accurate reflection of my loss than some of the day-to-day "carrying on" that we inevitably do.

The other thing that struck me was the passage of time. I found myself fumbling around with dates—how could the diagnosis be way back in 2011 if we're in 2014? My brain could hardly process the concept of years, plural, gone by. The trauma of it all can give the experience an ever-present quality still, with the interesting effect or, I suppose, illusion that we have a closer temporal connection to you too. And that is all I want—a sense of closeness and connection. So to realize that in fact time is passing, that the pictures of you reflect moments that are becoming more deeply set in my history day by day—well, this can feel horribly sad and threatening. Time seems to heal only in a superficial sense; I may be living a new normal with more joy and less acute anguish, but the feeling of distance produces a new pain.

Assuming I have some years left on this planet, I will only learn more and more what the passage of time will do to my grief. For now, I must remember to stand back and look at life from a wider angle which reveals that from the universe's standpoint we have existed in the same moment, and that our DNA links us inextricably together, always.

Living Beyond

Coda

I am not killed
Yet do not feel the stronger for it, rather
Vastly changed.
My counter to Mr. Nietzsche
May just be semantic,
But the only unquestionable choice remaining
Is in how I might proceed.
For the moment I am here,
Mortally wounded,
Learning to be brave.

March 23, An Address on Grieving...

North Chapel, Woodstock, Vermont

THANK YOU FOR ANOTHER OPPORTUNITY to speak with you. Last May when I stood here, I was about seven months out from the loss of my son Ryland. In some ways his death feels just as recent and searing; traumatic events seem to retain a sort of immediacy that makes it hard to compute the passage of time. But time does march along, perhaps nowhere best evident than in the busy pursuits of my nine-month-old Silas, who was just a part of me last spring. So I am grateful for another moment to pause and reflect a little on where I am now, to perhaps clarify my answer to that question, "how are you?", a question which tends to make me stumble and wonder if I will ever have a straightforward reply. I am not an expert on loss, simply a reporter on my own heart who is fortunate to have this loving space to share some observations. And I do so with the understanding that everyone has a story of loss, and for some folks here that story may be quite fresh and stirring and difficult. My hope is that stories shared may collectively do a bit of healing.

When I think back on my life before this most transforming experience of losing a child, I begin to see the irony that I would actually find myself in this position to speak about loss in a meaningful way. Truthfully, I was never a fan of the topic. I favored predictability and order—a place for everything, and everything reliably in its place. I was a kid who took pleasure in dusting her shelves and arranging everything back in a certain way, which I would care to interpret less as OCD and more as a precocious "Feng shui" sensibility. But no matter, my family could certainly testify to my "organized" nature and how losing simple objects could send me into a tailspin.

Growing up, my family was not immune from losses far larger and more tragic. My mother lost her biological father when she was two and her mother when I was three. My father lost his brother, my uncle, during my adolescent years. Yes, cancer had wreaked havoc quite enough. But these events did not make me want to look loss any more squarely in the eye, which is probably not a comfort zone for a child or teenager anyway, nor for the broader culture for that matter. No, I still worked to keep the chaos at bay, as if this were achievable.

Fast forward to graduate school in social work, and even there I shied away from courses on death, dying and bereavement. I had no problem plunging into all other forms of complicated human situations—familial strife and behavioral disorders and emotional crises. In other words, the stuff of life. And my passion for this work came from a personal conviction about suffering: that we can go to dark places and come back stronger for it, and that sometimes people just need a little support and understanding on that journey.

I do not discount those beliefs now but I am forced to revisit the old adage "what doesn't kill you makes you stronger." Ryland's illness and death cast many things in new light, adding dimension and shadow that were not visible before. What if an event occurs that is so unbearable that it does, in essence, kill you? The phrase becomes "what does kill you changes you" and the question becomes: How do you rebuild? Maybe I've been surrounded by young children too long but I can't get the image of Humpty Dumpty out of my head. Eventually in life, we probably all have a great fall, and all the king's horses and men cannot save you. The saving is up to you with the help of loved ones and kind strangers and those influences you wish to help mold you back into shape. There will be pieces of your original self, pieces discarded and pieces added, with the effect of being recognizable but not the same, like some fractured Picasso version of Humpty Dumpty that you will learn to live with and hopefully love.

And here is the tough part about profound grief, at least from my experience so far: Unlike other struggles, you don't arrive at some victorious point of overcoming, you don't close the door firmly on all the pain and move on feeling empowered for having survived. Certainly there are elements of our saga that are now behind us—the insane decision making and medical situations. And there are clear signs that many joys that had been lost for a long while have returned to our lives such as music and movies and the pleasure of a good meal. But a loss like this stays like a deep wound that may never fully heal, creating a lasting and pervasive vulnerability. The triggers are woven into our lives in expected and unexpected ways—in photographs and old toys, in songs and expressions. Memories can flood in at any given moment which, when involving a child and terminal illness, can still bring back the helplessness and horror. And while some of these concrete images and things may be particularly evocative, I find that Ryland has a more amorphous and constant presence for me, in a way that infuses life with chronic longing and wondering about who he would be now. Where time does any kind of healing, a creeping sense of distance from the last moments together can bring on fresh pain.

Somehow the pain and sadness of all this can commingle with remarkable joy, in a way that makes me wonder if any of these emotional states can ever really exist in distinct, pure form. I think of the image of little Silas learning how to handle a ball and realize the orange sparkly ball he is playing with was a gift to Ryland from the radiation team at Dartmouth. Such a scene can bring a flood of grim and dire memories, but also waves of gratitude for the people who cared for Ryland and waves of joy for this new little child delighting in innocent play. The brain has to do some acrobatics just to take it all in. I think of the image of Jane and Silas sitting on the living room rug together, each engaged in their own age-appropriate play but still connecting with one another through looks and squeals. So much heartache that Jane lost the dear playmate who was so much closer in age paired with so much hope that she will have a close and beautiful bond, albeit different, with her littlest brother. These are the kinds of moments that fill my days and that might make me give you a paralyzed blank look when responding to "how are you?"

I tend to be so many things at once.

If grief has taught me anything, if I have found any shred of relief or maybe even growth in this experience, it has been in the necessary willingness to surrender to life and to the whole emotional concert as much as possible. Life is the music and you are the dancer, and the more you can synchronize, the more natural the dance. You may have some artistic license when it comes to choreography, but always with an ear for the music, which may change and surprise you and force you to move in unexpected ways. Both my son's illness and the grieving process have had lives of their own in which I could participate but not control. I have been forced to allow the most unacceptable events and emotions ride their course. The strength comes not in ever feeling solid again, but in learning that you can somehow live with such an intense wound, and that you may break again and again but so too can you reassemble the pieces.

This is a distinctly different life than that of an organized, type A-ish individual with visions and plans for the future, for the social worker who thought she had landed safely in the "helper" role. I mourn for her lost innocence.

But Ryland has most likely taken me to a place that is more real and authentic and connected to the human experience, with so many opposing forces and dimensions and emotional experiences bound up together. I will need his example of courage to dwell here, and that is a word I have found particularly appealing. There is probably good reason we have had this quote from a fortune cookie up on our fridge since the days of his illness: "Courage is rightly considered the foremost of the virtues, for upon it all others depend" (a quote from Winston Churchill). Even more generally, it seems, courage needs to be a foremost part of living, with its inevitable losses and changes and heartbreak.

For me, the word courage does not feel flashy or valiant. It feels more quiet and tender than that. Perhaps it is its Latin root ('cor', meaning 'heart') coming through that makes me think of going into battle, not with a shield but with your gaping wounds exposed, trusting that you will survive. So too do we open up to our life experiences with courage. Not unlike opening our doors during March in Vermont, not knowing if you will find unrelenting cold or a dismal "wintry mix" or perhaps a euphoric blast of warm sun accompanied by bird calls. The changes may make us all crazy at times, but we also know it wouldn't be March without them. It is, after all, the contrast that makes the different experiences so powerfully felt. May our collective courage help us to live out these very full human lives, with all their disparate and challenging moments, may it nourish the growth of lasting bonds between us, and may it inspire us to hold fast in heart and mind the courageous example of loved ones gone before.

August 3...

It's been a while since I've written—not a reflection of any less thought about you Ryland. Am I avoiding the added emotion that writing can bring out? Is it more simply the increased business of life with a toddler? I don't know. But here we are in August. We are in Rhode Island for another summer visit without you. You would be five years old, and I think of all the things you would be doing now—such a big boy. Jane, of course, is a big girl herself at seven. Meanwhile, Silas, at one, is just getting started, and we are back to the constant effort of trying to support his need to move and learn and also protect him from harm! He's not walking yet but he's plenty mobile, and with a will that has been getting stronger and stronger. It's been fun to introduce him to more things and expand his world beyond the home. As I watched him delight in the activities at the Montshire Museum, it struck me that I did feel a real joy at seeing him get a foothold in the world. Maybe we have become more reinvested in life's offerings than I thought, despite the giant hole we will always live with.

I have had the strange experience, a couple times recently, where I've explained to someone I've just met that I lost a child. Typically this happens when someone observes the gap between Jane and Silas and wonders if there's another one. I don't really hesitate to explain—it's not something I feel I need to hide. But it is bizarre to talk about it as matter of fact, and as something a little further back in history, with the effect of this emotional disconnect that can in some ways feel like relief, and in some ways feel so misrepresentative of the emotional impact and legacy. I guess it will always be so that the real grief lives in more private and intimate places. There was the moment a few weeks ago when I was in your room with Silas and I spotted something behind the bed. It was the tractor piece of the farm-themed puzzle that I had out in the room, missing its one, most treasured part. As I held that piece, I was overcome with the full intensity of my sadness, which is such a full-body, physical feeling. I thought how it probably ended up behind the bed because you had been playing with it, representing a now rare sort of unexpected reminder and piece of evidence of your physical life with us. You felt so close and yet so terribly far all at once. How fitting that it should be a tractor too, an object for which your brother shares the same delight and enthusiasm. We have a complete farm puzzle now but you, my dear, will always be my life's missing piece.

Yellow Blanket

Jessica Stout

You wore a yellow blanket when you took your leave,
a choice made in the moment, both quick and intentional.
Was it the thick softness, a final gesture of comfort and holding?
Or was it that color that drew me,
like a lost insect in the dark.

The half moon could only illuminate the night so much,
yet bright yellow is the color of your goodbye.
It is a visual burst that stands up to the immense sorrow of that scene,
seared into my memory;
a parting gift that offers healing associations
that weave your light into my days.

Sun, fire—you urge us to grow, to stay warm and soft.
And train the eye to see light in dark places.
And guide us to those states of grace
that turn absence into presence.

Red Wagon

I take young Silas for a ride in a red wagon
Made entirely of plastic,
But a clever design nonetheless,
With swiveling wheels,
A serviceable handle,
And two moveable seats fore and aft.

The little boy loves to exploit
Those latter possibilities,
Folding one seat up, the other down,
And back again,
Splaying himself across the length of the deck,
As I labor to pull him up, down, and over
The terrain around his home.

I did this before with his older brother,
Gone from us a while now,
But with the greater challenge
I feel in the current pulling,
The question arises:
Is it simply a matter of my own diminished strength,
Or somehow, by some mysterious agency,
The presence of two grandsons
Together in the red wagon?

March 7...

DEAR RYLAND,

I see now you are my guide: how to live step by step, one foot in the seen world of doing and routine and one foot in that place of vast mystery, of connection to you through the portal of my broken heart. Is there even a line between the two? Life is so big and layered, not to be grabbed with a vice grip but engaged with the flexibility of a yogi, it seems. A grief story has no end, but let me close this moment with infinite gratitude to you, my little shaman. May your life continue to inspire our own and remind us to stretch our hearts and minds to be as fully human as we can be.

Epilogue

The creation of this book naturally required significant time spent with the content. Would I have revisited these difficult memories and moments so soon or so thoroughly? Probably not. I came up against my own resistance quite a bit as I undertook the challenge of reading my own story and re-experiencing the painful details therein. But I took my time with it, and ultimately came away so grateful to have a record and hopeful that it will serve a purpose.

There was also something deeply healing about engaging in a creative process with my father, whose skill both in visual art and with the written word has always been so impressive and moving to me. I could not have foreseen the evolution of a joint endeavor such as this, notwithstanding the profound wish that there had been no reason to produce such a book in the first place! But if Ryland had to leave us, I am forever grateful that his Poppi, my dad, had the courage to channel our grief and our love in this way, to work with an altogether different and most challenging medium for the sake of honoring our beloved boy's life.

As I reflected on my own accounting, I was struck by the recurring sentiment that our loss was "unbearable." No doubt this was how I felt—there is no exaggeration here. But I cannot help but notice that I am in fact here, alive, breathing, reading these words. Moreover, I can say I even know joy as more that just an occasional part of life. My daughter Jane delights me with her passions and open-hearted approach to life. My third-born, Silas, has me in stitches much of the time with his goofy energy and exuberance. And my husband, Matt, and I have somehow, together, climbed out of the abyss enough to reclaim various life pleasures that feed our souls and fortify our relationship.

I still, of course, think of Ryland all of the time, and the pain of his absence is still very real. However, I have come to understand that humans can indeed bear tremendous burdens. I'm not sure if it's a trait we are born with, one that we uncover as life demands, or if it's a capacity we develop when necessary. But to those in the throes of the "unbearable" I can affirm with compassion and conviction: You are built to survive.

About the Authors

Jessica Stout has a professional background in clinical social work, with a focus on children and families in mental health settings. She holds a BA in Psychology from Connecticut College and an MSW from Columbia University. In recent years, Jessica has been a full time parent, a role encompassing great joys as well as the profound sorrow of losing her middle child to a terminal illness. A life-changing experience, this loss has prompted Jessica's deep exploration of human grief and confirmed, for her, the cathartic and illuminating power of the written word.

Walter Horak is a professional sculptor who exhibits widely and whose work is represented in numerous public and private collections throughout the United States and abroad. During his career as a visual artist, Walter has held teaching positions that have ranged from primary grades through the college level. He holds an undergraduate degree from Harvard and graduate degrees from the Rhode Island School of Design and University of Massachusetts Dartmouth. He resides in Rhode island.

Ira Byock, MD is a leading palliative care physician and public advocate for improving care through the end of life. He serves as Executive Director and Chief Medical Officer for the Institute for Human Caring of Providence Health and Services, based in Torrance, CA. Dr. Byock is Professor at the Geisel School of Medicine at Dartmouth. He served as Director of Palliative Medicine at Dartmouth-Hitchcock Medical Center in Lebanon, New Hampshire from 2003 through July 2013.

Dr. Byock has authored numerous articles on the ethics and practice of care. His research led to conceptual frameworks for the lived experience of advanced illness, subjective quality of life measures, and effective life-completion counseling. His leadership in development of groundbreaking prototypes for concurrent care of people through the end of life has been foundational to advancing patient-centered care. More information is available at Ira.Byock.org

Acknowledgments

GIVEN OUR UTTER LACK OF EXPERIENCE IN BOOK CRAFT, we feel a special necessity to cite the people who lent key support to our fledgling efforts. These were individuals who spent time with the manuscript and encouraged us to move forward, in spite of its difficult subject matter and unusual, dual author format. Ira Byock deserves special mention, not only for his contribution to the book but especially for his wise and compassionate care in the darkest of days. Reverend Daniel Jantos offered us comparably deep nourishment. Rosemary Lonborg of the Jimmy Fund, Saul Wisnia at Dana Farber, authors Laura Claridge and Dawn Tripp, Kermit Hummel at Countryman Press, friends Marv Klassen-Landis, Dr. James Everett, Cathleen Everett and Rich Higgins were all clear voices in their advice to us. Thanks to Elizabeth Rinkel for her tech help. Sonja Hakala, from Full Circle Press, guided us expertly every step of the way in the publishing process, and in that process became a friend.

And we would be remiss if we did not here salute, again, that legion of people who helped us in myriad ways during our fateful year with Ryland: doctors and clinicians at Dartmouth-Hitchcock Medical Center, notably Dr. Jack van Hoff who is the Section Chief of Pediatric Hematology/Oncology at Dartmouth-Hitchcock Clinic in Lebanon, New Hampshire, and other professionals from the at-large medical community who consulted on the case, the community of Woodstock, friends and family spread all over the country, strangers who managed to say or do the right thing at the right time, individuals conveying concern without fear or embarrassment, and others who had the grace to be silent and just be with us.

Faithful aunts and uncles, from near and far, were unwavering in their efforts to be there, one way or another, for Ryland and the whole family. Daughter, Sister, and Aunt Natasha Horak filled her nephew's life with creativity and, with this book's cover, created a lasting visual tribute to him. Richard Epstein, steadfast friend all the while, provided Ryland some of the sweetest moments of care in those final, difficult days.

We were never alone in the struggle, realizing of course that no one facing this kind of loss should ever have to be. At one especially difficult point in his treatment, Ryland urged, "Be careful everyone," an admonishment taken to heart when we now acknowledge the need to always be full of care for one another.

And finally, we express profound gratitude to that intimate circle of loved ones who have stood firmly with us, not only for this bookmaking but also throughout all the chapters of a continuing family story. To Nonni, who has offered unfailing support and nurturance in her roles as wife, mother, and grandmother. Likewise Grandma Julie for imparting her boundless love and positive energy when it was sorely needed. Above all to Matt and Jane, who loved Ryland constantly, joyfully, unconditionally and who continue to celebrate his life and abiding place in our hearts. And to Silas, who, by some fateful measure, needed to join our wounded tribe and bring to it his own infectious, healing spirit. In time, dear boy, you will come to know your big brother and the strength of a familial bond, unseen but unbroken.

SELECTED READINGS

Ira Byock, *Dying Well*, 1997, Riverhead Books

Ira Byock, *The Four Things That Matter Most*, 2004, Atria Books

Ira Byock, *The Best Care Possible*, 2012, Penguin Group

Pema Chodron, *When Things Fall Apart*, 1997, Shambhala Publications

Atul Gawande, *Being Mortal*, 2014, Profile Books Ltd.

Joan Halifax, *Being with Dying,* 2008, Shambhala Publications

Martha Whitmore Hickman, *Healing After Loss*, 1994, HarperCollins

Ann Hood, *Comfort*, 2008, W.W. Norton Company, Inc.

Elisabeth Kübler-Ross and David Kessler, *Life Lessons*, 2000 Scribner

Stephen and Ondrea Levine, *Who Dies?*, 1982, Anchor Books

C.S. Lewis, *A Grief Observed*, C.S. Lewis Pte Ltd 1961

The poem "Kindness", Naomi Shihab Nye, *The Words Under the Words: Selected Poems*, 1995, Eighth Mountain Press

Emily Rapp, *The Still Point of the Turning World*, 2013 Penguin

Rebecca Solnit, *Field Guide to Getting Lost*, 2005, Penguin

The poem "There was a Child went Forth", Walt Whitman, *Leaves of Grass*, first published in 1855

Terry Tempest Williams, *Refuge*, 1991, Pantheon

CPSIA information can be obtained at www.ICGtesting.com
Printed in the USA
BVOW05s0348110716

454869BV00002B/8/P